D1566794

MUSICAL ICONOGRAPHY

MUSICAL ICONOGRAPHY: A MANUAL FOR CATALOGUING

MUSICAL SUBJECTS IN WESTERN ART BEFORE 1800

Howard Mayer Brown and Joan Lascelle

Harvard University Press, Cambridge, Massachusetts, 1972

© Copyright 1972 by the President and Fellows of Harvard College
All rights reserved
Library of Congress Catalog Card Number 76-180151
SBN 674-59220-4
Printed in the United States of America

ML
111
. B825
M9

PREFACE

Like many who are interested in the history of musical instruments and their uses, the authors of this handbook have been collecting reproductions of works of art with musical subjects for a number of years, although in a completely unsystematic fashion. We have been frustrated in our attempts to use collections of random objects because neither of us has known how to arrange their contents in an orderly way. Our primitive systems of locating material within them have been incomplete and inconsistent, so that many times we could not find all of the information needed when we looked for it, and objects once found were almost immediately lost. Moreover, the possibility of exchanging or sharing material with other scholars seemed remote, for if we could not control our own small groups of objects--we did not really know what we had—how could we arrange to share material profitably? These frustrations led to discussions about the kinds of questions that musical scholars can hope to answer using pictorial evidence and about methods of cataloguing art works so that the most useful information is quickly and easily available, and finally to our decision to form at the University of Chicago a modest Index of Musical Iconography. But we soon found that not a single work of art could be catalogued until we had devised a system applicable to all works of art. The present handbook explains that system.

We decided to begin the Index with the objects found in our own casually formed collections and add to them the pictorial sources already best known to musicologists. Thus, we began to catalogue the reproductions published in the standard anthologies of music in pictures, for example, Georg Kinsky, *A History of Music in Pictures* (London, 1930), Alexander Buchner, *Musical Instruments Through the Ages* (London, 1956), Frank L. Harrison and Joan Rimmer, *European Musical Instruments* (New York, 1965), Karl Michael Komma, *Musikgeschichte in Bildern* (Stuttgart, 1961), and so on. We soon found, however, that these anthologies often do not supply enough information to evaluate the pictures properly as musicological evidence. Therefore, our first project had to be modified; we began the Index by cataloguing reproductions found in art historical books, museum catalogues, and so on, most of them related in some way to the reproductions in the standard anthologies. In the meantime the funds which enabled Miss Lascelle to work

ALMA COLLEGE
MONTEITH LIBRARY
ALMA, MICHIGAN

on the Index ran out, so that its rate of expansion has slowed down. Nevertheless, I intend to continue the Index by searching exhaustively through various limited bodies of material, for example, the Italian Renaissance paintings listed in the bibliographies by Bernard Berenson, the reproductions of art works in the Max Epstein Archive of The University of Chicago, illuminated manuscripts described in various museum and library catalogues, and so on.

Just as Miss Lascelle and I pooled our randomly assembled collections to begin the Index, we pooled our ideas to form the system by which the Index operates. Each of us has contributed equally to the system. Nevertheless, we each took initial responsibility for various parts of it. Miss Lascelle devised the method for classifying pictures of instruments by their shapes; she made up the first sets of assumed details and variable features; and she devised the initial lists of schools and media or types of objects. I felt myself responsible for suggesting the kinds of information that I believed musicologists would want to know about works of art and their subject matters. And I am largely responsible for the specific wording and the arrangement of the material in this handbook. The appendices, on the other hand, wrote themselves: they are simply examples of our method and lists taken from the Index of Musical Iconography.

Throughout the process of developing the system, we have criticized and revised each other's work until we could agree on a compromise form. The outlines that resulted from these discussions served as our cataloguing manual for a year. During this trial run, we reworked and expanded our preliminary outlines until we arrived at the system described in this book—a system that has worked for any object we have so far wished to catalogue and any information we have so far wished to retrieve.

We have two goals in mind in publishing this book. First, we wish to save others the time and effort of devising a workable cataloguing system for their own collections. Secondly, by making a ready-made system available, we would like to promote standardization of cataloguing and therefore cooperation among scholars working in this field. I would stress that the system outlined in the following pages need not be accepted in all of its particulars to be useful to other scholars. Our system is workable without any special equipment: following our rules, anyone with a pencil, a piece of paper, and a photograph can begin to build an archive. But we wished also to accommodate the needs of those interested in the advances of modern technology. The collector who wishes to use computers will have to change some of our procedures, but he can nevertheless take over much of our system without modification. The Index in Chicago will probably remain relatively small, just large enough to serve as a tool for research by one person or a small group of people. Some of our procedures have doubtless been influenced by that fact. For example, locator symbols, described in chapter III, are helpful for finding material without going to the cross-reference files in a relatively small collection. Someone forming a very large collection might find locator symbols cumbersome and ambiguous; simple accession numbers might better identify individual objects. Yet most of our procedures can still be taken over without modification. Moreover, collectors can easily broaden the scope of our Index to include Western art after 1800 and non-Western art of all periods by adding new classifications based on our principles. In short, we have attempted to invent a system for collecting pictures and retrieving information from them which is both flexible and clear enough to enable collectors with various interests and needs to adapt it relatively easily. If our handbook seems at first overly complicated, I urge the reader to withhold judgment until he has actually catalogued a few works of art. The rules in the following pages are admittedly intricate, but we feel that they are as simple as they can be and still supply the minimum amount of information required to use art works intelligently as musicological evidence. The table of contents has been made detailed enough to serve as both guide and checklist for cataloguing musical subjects in Western art before 1800 once the principles of the system, explained in the body of the text, have been mastered.

We are very grateful to the National Endowment for the Humanities for a grant which enabled us to begin our work on the Index and to the Research Committee of the Division of the Humanities at The University of Chicago for further grants. Without their material assistance we could not have made so much progress so quickly.

In the early stages of formulating our system we were encouraged by the example of the Index of Christian Art at Princeton University, and, although the keepers of that Index do not know it, we owe them a debt of gratitude. We are also indebted to Cynthia L. Clark, Director of Section of Slides and Photographs, Department of Art and Archaeology, Princeton University, who kindly provided us with a copy of that collection's classification system which proved to be very helpful; in fact, we adapted some portions of it for our own system. And many of our categories of subject entries, such as the type and placement of performers, the location and occasion of performances, and so on, were first suggested by Emanuel Winternitz in *Musical Instruments and Their Symbolism in Western Art* (New York, 1967). But we are most deeply in debt to Ruth Philbrick, Curator of the Max Epstein Archive of The University of Chicago, and to Phyllis Unosawa, Assistant Curator of the same collection. They have patiently and graciously answered our countless questions about the theory and practice of picture collections and about the specific problems raised by individual pictures, and they have contributed their duplicate material to our collection whenever it has contained musical subject matter. Their help and guidance have been, and will continue to be, of invaluable aid to us and to all future users of the Index. And we are grateful to Robert Williams, who very kindly made the elegant line drawings of instrument shapes in chapter XIV; and to Carol Garlington, who bravely supervised the transformation of the manuscript into a book.

Finally, I should like to thank all of the people who read through the manuscript and made helpful suggestions and criticisms: Edmund Bowles, David Boyden, Lenore Coral, Frederick Crane, Greer Garden, Dagmar Groeneveld, Harald Heckmann, Helen Hollis, Cynthia Hoover, James McKinnon, Walter Salmen, H. Colin Slim, and Emanuel Winternitz.

An event of some importance for the study of musical subjects in works of art took place in August 1971, too late to be mentioned in chapter I. At a conference of the International Association of Music Libraries in St. Gall, Switzerland, a new organization was formed, the Répertoire international d'iconographie musicale (RIdIM) under the direction of Mme. la comtesse de Chambure, Barry Brook, and Harald Heckmann. This body has set as its task the supervision of a systematic attempt to collect and catalogue all works of art with musical subject matter. Let us hope that the group will stimulate international cooperation and that many more picture collections will soon be available to workers in the field.

Howard Mayer Brown

Chicago, Illinois
November 1971

CONTENTS

ILLUSTRATIONS

MUSICAL ICONOGRAPHY

I.
WHAT CAN WORKS OF ART TEACH US ABOUT MUSIC?

Was lehren uns die Bildwerke? What can works of art teach us about music, in particular about musical instruments and their place in the civilizations of the Middle Ages and the Renaissance? In the years that have passed since Hugo Leichtentritt asked that question,[1] some progress has been made in answering it, and yet there is still no central index of pictorial sources, nor any agreement among scholars about the methods of organizing and evaluating works of art as musicological evidence.[2] But the need to investigate musical subjects in art has long been recognized by scholars and performers. The subject was discussed

1. Hugo Leichtentritt, "Was lehren uns die Bildwerke des 14.-17. Jahrhunderts über die Instrumentalmusik ihrer Zeit?" *Sammelbände der internationalen Musikgesellschaft* 7 (1905-06), 315-365.
2. For some examples of the way musical scholars have used iconographical evidence with excellent results, see David Boyden, *The History of Violin Playing from Its Origins to 1761* (London: Oxford University Press, 1965); Valentin Denis, *De Muziekinstrumenten in de Nederlanden en in Italië naar hun Afbeelding in de 15e-eeuwsche Kunst* (Antwerp: Vitgeversmij. N. V. Standaard-Boekhandel, 1944); Reinhold Hammerstein, *Die Musik der Engel* (Bern and Munich: Francke Verlag, 1962); and Emanuel Winternitz, *Musical Instruments and Their Symbolism in Western Art* (New York: W. W. Norton, 1967). The last named work contains two essays of special interest to readers of this manual, "The Visual Arts as a Source for the Historian of Music" (pp. 25-42), and "The Knowledge of Musical Instruments as an Aid to the Art Historian" (pp. 43-56).
  At least three projects, differing in method, have been started to meet the lack of a central index. The "Commission internationale pour l'iconographie des instruments de musique" published a set of index cards without illustrations, *Iconographie des instruments de musique*, ed. D. F. Scheurleer (The Hague, 1914), but its work was stopped by World War I and never resumed.
  Albert Hess started the Archive of Music Representations in the Visual Arts, limited to Italian paintings and drawings of the fourteenth to the seventeenth centuries, at the Duluth branch of the University of Minnesota, and he published one volume of a projected series, *Italian Renaissance Paintings with Musical Subjects: A Corpus of Such Works in American Collections with Detailed Descriptions of the Musical Features*, Fascicle Eleven [sic] (New York, 1955). For a discussion of the archive and an explanation of its method, see Albert G. Hess, "The Cataloging [sic] of Music in the Visual Arts," *Notes* 11 (1953-54), 527-542; and for a critique of the only volume of illustrations issued, see Emanuel Winternitz's review in *Notes* 12 (1954-55), 598-600.
  An index of the reproductions in books of instruments in western European art from the Middle Ages to about 1800 was begun at The University of California at Berkeley in 1955 under the general direction of David Boyden. A sample of the work done there was distributed at the meeting of the Eighth Congress of the International Musicological Society

at the congresses of the International Musicological Society at Basel in 1906, at Paris in 1914, and at New York in 1961, at a combined meeting of the Society for Music in the Liberal Arts College, the American Musicological Society, and the Music Library Association at Rochester in 1951, and at the annual meeting of the American Musicological Society at New Orleans in 1966.[3] In 1929 Eric Blom said that "it should one day become possible to see portraits of any musician, pictures of any instrument and pictorial representations of all sorts of musico-historical events at a moment's notice,"[4] and since then scholars and performers have repeatedly pointed out their dependence on pictorial, literary, and other nonmusical sources in solving the problems of early performance practice. Frank Harrison, for example, writes:

> Of the kinds of evidence that exist for our period [1100-1450]—written music, archives and chronicles, iconography and imaginative writing—only the first has as yet been investigated systematically in depth . . . The written music of any time represents only the top of the iceberg that stands for musical events as a whole . . . For the centuries under discussion, it is particularly instrumental practice outside the church that belongs to the invisible part of the iceberg. Evidence about it cannot be direct, but indirect evidence may be drawn from comparable practices of the unwritten traditions where they still exist, as well as from documents and depictions properly evaluated.[5]

If pictorial evidence is to be used in musical research, art works that include representations of musical instruments, performances, notation, and so on must be systematically collected and catalogued, since conclusions about the common practices of a time must be based on as large a sampling of the sources as possible. For this reason we have established at the University of Chicago an index of musical iconography comprising musical subjects in Western art before 1800. Our initial task was to invent a system for cataloguing works of art that would

in New York in 1961. See Sydney R. Charles and David Boyden, "Musical Instruments in Paintings: An Index to Reproductions of Fourteenth-Century Italian Paintings Showing Musical Instruments," (mimeographed) (Berkeley, Calif., 1961).

3. See Hugo Leichtentritt, "Aeltere Bildwerke als Quellen der musikgeschichtlichen Forschung," *Bericht über den zweiten Kongress der Internationalen Musikgesellschaft zu Basel* (Leipzig: Breitkopf und Härtel, 1907), pp. 230-234; Emanuel Winternitz, "The Visual Arts as a Source for the Historian of Music," International Musicological Society, *Report of the Eighth Congress, New York 1961,* ed. Jan La Rue (Cassel: Bärenreiter, 1961), I, 109-120; and the summary of the discussion in New York, ibid., II, 84-87. Apparently no report of the congress in Paris in 1914 was ever published.

According to Hess, "Cataloging of Music," p. 528, musical iconography was discussed in Martin Bernstein, "Visual Aids in College Music Teaching," *Information Sheet of the Society for Music in the Liberal Arts College,* vol. 3, no. 1 (n.d.), suppl. 5, p. 3.

Since 1966 there have been several discussion groups at national meetings of the American Musicological Society devoted to the problems of iconographical research.

4. Introduction by Eric Blom to Georg Kinsky, ed., *A History of Music in Pictures* (London: J. M. Dent and Sons, 1930), p. viii.

5. Frank L. Harrison, "Tradition and Innovation in Instrumental Usage 1100-1450," *Aspects of Medieval and Renaissance Music,* ed. Jan La Rue (New York: W. W. Norton, 1966), pp. 320-321.

enable a musical scholar to answer the questions most relevant to his work as quickly and easily as possible, and one that could be used by anyone anywhere because it is formed of ordinary language rather than codes or cryptic abbreviations. The need for such a cataloguing system has been pressing, because until standardized procedures can be applied to each artistic monument the sources cannot be adequately controlled bibliographically and until some agreement is reached about the method and terminology for gathering, evaluating, and describing evidence, the perennial dream of cooperation among scholars cannot be realized. In devising a cataloguing system, we have had to ask ourselves constantly the first question—*Was lehren uns die Bildwerke?*—in order to guarantee that our system, complicated as it must be, is nevertheless the simplest and clearest way to isolate the information that musical scholars will need in their research.

Works of art can furnish scholars with three principal kinds of evidence. They can help to answer questions dealing with the history and construction of musical instruments, questions relating to the performance of earlier music, and questions about the relationship of music to the culture at large. Each of these areas--organological, practical, and cultural-historical--requires a slightly different approach to the individual work of art.

The scholar using pictures as organological evidence must keep in mind that the instruments may not be correctly drawn and that even the most accurate pictures cannot tell certain details of construction, such as the material from which an instrument is made, the size and shape of a bore, the thickness of a soundboard, or the tension of a string. Yet despite these inherent deficiencies, works of art are still our best source of information on the history, construction, and playing techniques of early instruments. Conclusions about instruments drawn from pictorial evidence can sometimes be corroborated by literary or archival sources, but written records alone often tell us little because we frequently do not know to which sort of instrument one of the many, varied literary terms applies. Only when we find a picture in which an instrument is labeled, or one which is accompanied by a text which includes the name of the instrument illustrated, can we be certain that we know what kind of instrument was meant by that name at that time.[6]

The importance of pictures is due not only to the ambiguity of the written sources, but to the lack of extant early instruments. Very few musical instruments survive from before 1500. And the relatively small number of sixteenth-century specimens to be found in museums and private collections throughout the world probably cannot be considered a representative cross section of the instruments then in use, for the ravages of time and the peculiar natures

6. The subject entry "Instrument, reference to [Instrument name]" controls this type of information in the Index of Musical Iconography. The technique of listing names of musical instruments and musical terms found in works of art or in the texts accompanying illustrations in manuscripts and printed books is explained in XIII.3.e below.

of collectors have almost certainly combined to preserve those examples that were exceptionally elegant, unusual, or structurally sound, while almost all instruments that were simply functional, commonplace, or frail have been lost. Sixteenth-century keyboard instruments, for example, are better represented in museum collections than wind instruments, and very few unrestored sixteenth-century lutes survive because of the inherent weaknesses in the structure of the instrument. Art works can show us not only how the instruments looked, but also how they were played. Paintings have furnished Edwin M. Ripin, for example, with crucial evidence about the history of double-manual harpsichords in early seventeenth-century Flanders.[7] Works of art can furnish strong evidence that specific instruments were used at a particular time and place even when literary, archival, and musical documents do not corroborate that conclusion.

There are, however, factors which may prevent the evidence offered by art works about the history and construction of instruments from being trusted to represent reality in the artist's own time. On the one hand, an artist's lack of skill or his ignorance of instruments may have prevented him from depicting them accurately. On the other hand, skill and knowledge notwithstanding, he may have had no intention of depicting an instrument of his own time. Artists may sometimes have copied an earlier source or artistic tradition, or wished to include ancient instruments in an historical scene, or modified or invented instruments for some intellectual or symbolic reason.

As might be expected, medieval artists normally depicted instruments more schematically than later artists. Werner Bachmann's *Die Anfänge des Streichinstrumentenspiels*,[8] a book which deals expertly with medieval art as musicological evidence, contains very few illustrations that could serve a modern instrument maker as models for reconstructions, because the medieval painters represented there did not include sufficient detail and were in any case not interested in revealing the functional structure of the objects they presented. Some modern makers have, on the other hand, based reconstructions of instruments on fifteenth-century paintings by Memling, van Eyck, and others. The instruments held by the angel musicians in Hubert and Jan van Eyck's famous *Ghent Altarpiece*,[9] dated 1432, for example, are shown with the clarity and precision of a photograph. A positive organ, a fiddle, or a frame harp built to resemble the ones in that painting would certainly function properly.

And yet it is not true, as is often assumed, that medieval art is necessarily less valuable as organological evidence than more realistic art. For by realistic

7. See Edwin M. Ripin, "The Two-Manual Harpsichord in Flanders Before 1650," *The Galpin Society Journal* 21 (1968), 33-39. For a similar article on clavichords, making use of iconographical material, see idem, "The Early Clavichord," *The Musical Quarterly* 53 (1967), 518-538.

8. Leipzig: Breitkopf und Härtel, 1964; translated into English by Norma Deane as *The Origins of Bowing* (London: Oxford University Press, 1968).

9. Reproduced in, among other places, Kinsky, *History of Music in Pictures*, pl. 56.

art, most of us mean photographic art—that is, objects drawn in correct perspective and modeled in light and shade to look three-dimensional. But by valuable organological evidence, we mean pictures of instruments drawn with accurate proportion and detail. Three-dimensionality is no more necessary to their accuracy than it is to an architect's drawing. There are, of course, many medieval pictures of instruments that are schematic and inaccurate. But there are also many later examples that are realistic and inaccurate, a well-known one being Grünewald's sixteenth-century *Isenheim Altar*,[10] in which the three-dimensional angels play recognizable, three-dimensional instruments, but both the instruments and the playing techniques are distorted. Conversely, although modern instrument makers have based reconstructions of instruments on fifteenth-century paintings by Memling and van Eyck, they could also reconstruct instruments from well-chosen earlier pictures, such as the harp in the eleventh-century manuscript from Corpus Christi College, Cambridge, shown in Galpin's *Old English Instruments of Music*.[11] The artist's skill, medium, scale, and goal have more to do with making a picture organologically valuable than the picture's date or style.

Therefore, medieval art must not be dismissed out of hand as musicological evidence. Even the most schematic representations can tell us some significant facts: the kinds of instruments in common use and some information about their construction and use, such as their approximate shapes and how they were held and played. Such conclusions must be based on as broad a sampling of the sources as possible, however, and even then accepted with some caution. But there is at least some hope that the histories of most instruments can eventually be written with the help of iconographical evidence. Emanuel Winternitz's essays on the lira da braccio and on the survival of the kithara and the evolution of the English cittern can serve as models of what such research incorporating iconographical evidence can accomplish.[12]

In using pictorial sources, the musical scholar must take care to investigate the possibility that the artist has depicted an instrument copied from an earlier artistic source and not from real life. The ninth-century "Utrecht Psalter," itself perhaps based on an earlier original, was copied several times in the eleventh

10. Reproduced in, among other places, Karl Michael Komma, *Musikgeschichte in Bildern* (Stuttgart: Alfred Kröner, 1961), no. 197.

11. Francis W. Galpin, *Old English Instruments of Music*, 4th ed., rev. Thurston Dart (London: Methuen, 1965), pl. 3.

12. "Lira da Braccio," in *Die Musik in Geschichte und Gegenwart*, vol. 8 (1960). (An extract, in English, from this article can be found in idem, *Musical Instruments and Their Symbolism*, pp. 86-98) and "The Survival of the Kithara and the Evolution of the English Cittern: A Study in Morphology," *Journal of the Warburg and Courtauld Institutes* 24 (1961), 222-229. The latter article can be found in idem, *Musical Instruments and Their Symbolism*, pp. 57-65; and a condensed version appears in *Music Libraries and Instruments*, Hinrichsen's Eleventh Music Book (London: Hinrichsen Edition, 1961), pp. 209-214.

and twelfth centuries.[13] Some representations of musical instruments were taken over with only minor changes into the newer versions, but others show more significant differences. Thus, the value of the pictures as organological evidence increases greatly when we know that they are copied and from what. Similarly, details of many other art works are merely copies from earlier works; indiscriminate reliance on them as evidence of contemporary reality is therefore unjustified.

In the Renaissance some artists painted scenes of classical antiquity and included pseudo-ancient instruments. The works of both Filippino Lippi and Piero di Cosimo abound in examples of musical instruments which cannot have been in common use in the sixteenth century—instruments invariably associated with neoclassical scenes. Some may well be more or less accurate representations of instruments in use during ancient times, perhaps copied from older artifacts. Yet often artists simply invented instruments in neoclassical shapes; many of them could never have existed because they are absurdly nonfunctional. Also, painters sometimes depicted those imaginatively designed mock pseudo-ancient instruments that were carried by actors in theatrical productions of the Renaissance, which often concealed functioning contemporary instruments or were playable themselves. Emanuel Winternitz discusses these shams in two essays: one on musical archaeology in Raphael's "Parnassus," and the other on the instruments in paintings by Filippino Lippi, Piero di Cosimo, and Lorenzo Costa.[14]

Occasionally an artist will modify the details of an instrument's construction for purely intellectual, artistic, or symbolic reasons. For example, the anonymous illuminator of Herrad of Landsberg's twelfth-century encyclopedia "Hortus deliciarum" shows King David carrying a triangular harp or psaltery with ten strings.[15] Both its shape and the number of its strings are likely to have been determined by the artist's desire to associate David with sacred

13. Utrecht, Universiteitsbibliotheek, MS 32. See E. T. DeWald, *The Illustrations of the Utrecht Psalter* (Princeton: Princeton University Press, [1932]). The later copies are: London, British Museum, MS Harley 603 (ca. 1000); Cambridge, Trinity College Library, MS R.17.1 (ca. 1147-1150); and Paris, Bibliothèque Nationale, MS lat. 8846 (ca. 1200). The Cambridge manuscript is published in a facsimile edition as *The Canterbury Psalter*, ed. M. R. James (London: Friends of Canterbury Cathedral, 1935).

14. Winternitz, "Archeologia musicale del rinascimento nel Parnasso di Raffaello," *Rendiconti della Pontifica Accademia Romana di Archeologia* 27 (1952-54), 359-388 (for an English translation, see "Musical Archeology of the Renaissance in Raphael's *Parnassus*," in *Musical Instruments and Their Symbolism*, pp. 185-201); and idem, "Instruments de musique étrange chez Filippino Lippi, Piero di Cosimo, et Lorenzo Costa," *Les fêtes de la renaissance* 1 (Paris: Centre national de la recherche scientifique, 1956), 379-395 (for an English translation, see "Musical Instruments for the Stage in Paintings by Filippino Lippi, Piero di Cosimo, and Lorenzo Costa," in *Musical Instruments and Their Symbolism*, pp. 211-215.

15. Reproduced in Herrad of Landsberg, *Hortus Deliciarum*, ed. Christian Moritz Engelhardt (Stuttgart and Tübingen: J. G. Cotta, 1818), pl. IV, and in idem, *Hortus Deliciarum*, ed. A. Straub and G. Keller (Strasbourg: Imprimerie Strasbourgeoise, 1899), pl. V bis; discussed in Hugo Steger, *David Rex et Propheta* (Nuremberg: Hans Carl, 1961), p. 233.

symbols– the triangle suggesting the Trinity and the number of strings, the Ten Commandments even though triangular instruments are not uncommon, and medieval psalters do refer to ten-stringed instruments. In short, even for the musical scholar who is interested solely in organological evidence, pictorial sources must be used with some caution; each picture must be studied in its artistic and historical context before it can be accepted as an illustration of contemporary reality.[16]

Composers in the Middle Ages and the Renaissance scarcely ever indicated that their music was written for specific groupings of instruments or voices. In some cases, perhaps, the performing forces were so conventional that no such indications were necessary: every musician would have known which instruments and voices the composer intended from the nature of the music. For example, Notre Dame organa in the twelfth and thirteenth centuries may normally have been performed by a more or less fixed ensemble of musicians. With other music, however, the composer seems not to have had in mind any specific sonority. He left to the performer the task of adapting the written notes to the acoustical environment, the social context, the forces available, and so on. On the one hand, then, modern scholars must rediscover lost conventions, and on the other, they must discern the limits within which earlier performers were free to interpret the music given them by the composer. Since the music manuscripts themselves do not supply answers to the sorts of questions about performance practice that later scores do, works of art and literary and archival documents, difficult as these are to interpret, must perforce constitute the principal sources for information about ensembles customarily used in performing earlier music.

Pictures can also reveal aspects of the social context of musical performances that would otherwise be difficult or impossible to discover. Works of art depicting real scenes show not only the number and kinds of performers and whether or not a conductor leads the group, but also the locations and occasions for musical performances, whether indoors or out, where the musicians sat or stood, whether or not an audience was present and, if so, where they sat, what the scenery for theatrical productions looked like, and what sorts of music were appropriate for weddings, funerals, civic and religious processions, and so on. Works of art reveal the sorts of occasions for which town bands played,[17] what musical forces were available to princes,[18] and even the extent

16. The musical scholar must also be cautious in assessing the present condition of paintings. Details of musical instruments are sometimes obscured by careless restoration. Mutilations of this sort occur more frequently in important paintings owned by large museums than in obscure works in small, provincial museums, too poor to afford extensive "restorations."

17. See, for example, François Lesure, *Musik und Gesellschaft im Bild* (Cassel: Bärenreiter, 1966), pls. 16, 55, and 66.

18. See, for example, Stanley Appelbaum, ed., *The Triumph of Maximilian I: 137 Woodcuts by Hans Burgkmair and Others* (New York: Dover, 1964).

to which professional musicians were joined by well-born amateurs in concerts at court.[19] And pictures are virtually the only evidence we shall ever have for discovering which musical accessories were used, when musicians played from written or printed music, when they used music stands, instrument cases, cheek bands, and so on.

If the student of organology needs to exercise caution in using pictorial evidence, anyone wishing to learn how music was performed during earlier times must be even more prudent in his use of works of art as evidence, for the questions they can answer depend entirely on the notion that artists depict contemporary reality. Thus, the extent to which an individual art work reflects true and common practice must be assessed before its testimony can be accepted as fact. The principal check on a picture's realism must come about through an evaluation of its subject matter. The precept that only scenes depicting real life can be said to illustrate reality may seem tautological, but it is the basic assumption which underlies the work of the careful musical iconographer.

The musical scholar must therefore concern himself with the intention of the artist, who often set out either to bring new life to a traditional iconographical program which had many fixed elements, or to illustrate a text which specified many of the details, including the number and kinds of musical instruments. Thus, the illumination in Herrad of Landsberg's twelfth-century "Hortus deliciarum," which shows three Sirens, one singing, while the other two play a transverse flute and a harp-psaltery, may illustrate a sermon by the theologian Honorius of Autun, who develops the allegory of the tempted Christian using the image of Ulysses and the Sirens.[20] Honorius equates the singing Siren with *avaricia* (covetousness), the flute, or "tybia," with *jactantia* (boastfulness), and the harp-psaltery, or "lira," with *luxuria* (lust). Thus, the picture may illustrate a specific text and furnish no information about the normal chamber ensembles of the twelfth century. Similarly, the traditional association of musical angels with the Virgin Mary very likely tells us little about musical practices in the Middle Ages and the Renaissance, although some scholars have based conclusions about fifteenth-century instrumentation on such angel consorts.[21]

19. See, for example, Heinrich Besseler, "Umgangsmusik und Darbietungsmusik im 16. Jahrhundert," *Archiv für Musikwissenschaft* 16 (1959), 21-43.

20. The three Sirens are reproduced in, among other places, Kinsky, *History of Music in Pictures*, pl. 35. The sermon is printed in Honorius of Autun, *Speculum Ecclesiae: Dominica in Septuagesima*, in J. P. Migne, ed., *Patrologiae Cursus Completus: Series Latina*, vol. 172 (Paris, 1895), cols. 855-856. For a more detailed exposition of the point that medieval artists and writers often fail to reflect reality, see James W. McKinnon, "Musical Instruments in Medieval Psalm Commentaries and Psalters," *Journal of the American Musicological Society* 21 (1968), 3-20.

21. See, for example, Curt Sachs, "Die Besetzung dreistimmiger Werke um das Jahr 1500," *Zeitschrift für Musikwissenschaft* 11 (1929), 386-389. The best work on angel musicians to date is Hammerstein, *Musik der Engel*.

Emile Mâle was the first person to show the extent to which manuscript illuminations, sculpture, and paintings, especially those created during the Middle Ages, depended on theatrical productions.[22] That is, some artists depicted scenes, particularly those derived from the Bible or from saints' lives, by showing contemporary theatrical representations of them, using as their model mystery and miracle plays. This practice aids the musical scholar, for even when an artist is illustrating a Biblical scene, if he copies a stage production he is in some sense depicting reality and his picture may then reveal normal musical practices. But the cautious musical iconographer must first take some pains to establish the connection of the work of art with theatrical convention.

Some artists illustrate traditional scenes by portraying mythical, Biblical, or historical figures in modern dress, and they, too, may therefore be depicting contemporary reality. Sixteenth-century paintings of the Prodigal Son, for example, often show him at the banquet table surrounded by his high-living companions. In such cases, there seems to be little reason to doubt that the artist was painting a situation that he himself might have seen in his own time. And similarly, fifteenth-century Netherlandish painters transpose Biblical events to their own time and place, so that their works can often be accepted as evidence of reality, although Netherlandish artists include disguised symbolism well into the eighteenth century.

The musical scholar must assure himself that the artist's choice of musical instruments does not depend entirely on a textual source, some form of symbolism, or on a traditional iconographical program only distantly related, if at all, to contemporary reality. The most solid iconographical evidence, of course, comes from paintings which illustrate contemporary events and which thus have almost the force of photographic reality. The many sixteenth-century works of art which show specific rulers in military activities and at courtly entertainments, coronations, weddings, and so on can presumably be accepted at face value as musicological evidence. Even one such painting is enormously useful in revealing performance practices.

These historical scenes can sometimes be found even before the sixteenth century: manuscript illuminations are a particularly rich source for them. Indeed, from the thirteenth century onward, the margins of the illuminated manuscripts are an especially fertile field of investigation for the musical iconographer, for they show, along with a host of grotesque creatures, beasts and birds, and angels and devils, some of whom spill over from the main miniatures, a number of quite ordinary people engaged in everyday activities— hunting, weaving, fighting, playing games, and making music.[23] The relation-

22. Emile Mâle, *L'Art religieux de la fin du moyen âge en France,* 3rd ed. (Paris: A. Colin, 1925).
23. The most detailed study to date of these marginalia is Lilian M. C. Randall, *Images in the Margins of Gothic Manuscripts* (Berkeley and Los Angeles: University of California Press, 1966).

ship of these marginal ornaments to the main miniatures, which usually embody a more traditional iconographic program or at least more clearly illustrate the accompanying text, is often problematical; art historians attempt, whenever they can, to show how the marginalia are linked with the overall plan of the page. Nevertheless, many of these everyday scenes can probably be accepted as straightforward musicological evidence, even though their connection with the real world must always remain in question and may one day be convincingly denied.

On the one hand, then, works of art show historical events and scenes from everyday life which seem to be factually true. It would be difficult to argue, for example, that the portraits of the Minnesinger in the fourteenth-century "Manessische Manuscript,"[24] many of whom are shown engaging in typical musical activities, or the minstrels in the thirteenth-century "Cantigas de Santa Maria"[25] do not represent at least some degree of reality, although the extent to which conclusions based on these miniatures alone can be applied beyond a very limited place and time remains an open question. On the other hand, pictures of angel concerts and mythological figures can scarcely ever constitute the major part of the evidence in any convincing argument about performing conventions, for such images are derived from literary sources or from tradition rather than from real life. A musical scholar who wishes to argue that in certain cases such scenes are based on contemporary theatrical productions himself bears the burden of proof for demonstrating that hypothesis. Unfortunately, the intent of many art works is not clear; they may well reveal actual performance practice, or they may merely illustrate some unknown text. The musical scholar must often make difficult decisions about the reliability of a work of art as musicological evidence, knowing that further research might reverse his decision. But such difficulties are an inherent part of the problem of dealing with pictorial sources, and the musical scholar must simply accustom himself to dealing with working hypotheses as well as with established fact.

Along with data about musical instruments and about performance practice, works of art also furnish information about the role of music in culture at large. Pictures not only help to explain the place of musical performances in society, but they also reveal characteristic ways in which musical subjects

24. Heidelberg, Universitätsbibliothek, MS Pal. germ. 848. The entire manuscript is reproduced in facsimile in *Manessische Lieder MS* (Leipzig: Insel Verlag, 1925-1927). Excerpts are reproduced in Hans Naumann, ed., *Die Minnesinger in Bildern der Manessischen Handschrift*, 2 vols. (Leipzig: Insel Verlag, n.d.).

25. Escorial, Biblioteca de San Lorenzo, MS J.b.2 and MS T.j.1; and Madrid, Biblioteca Nacional, MS 10069. The Madrid manuscript is published in facsimile in Julian Ribera y Tarragó, *La Música de las Cantigas: Estudio sobre su origen y naturaleza* (Madrid: Tipografía de la Revista de archivos, 1922). The musicians are also reproduced in Juan F. Riano *Critical and Bibliographical Notes on Early Spanish Music* (London: B. Quaritch, 1887).

were used symbolically or allegorically and how music was used to illuminate
the mythical, philosophical, theological, or educational doctrines of an age.
This aspect of iconography brings music into the sphere of cultural history
and, indeed, raises questions which relate more clearly to the latter discipline
than to music history as it has been narrowly conceived. One facet of music as
a part of cultural history, for example, will surely involve the frequent appear-
ance in works of art of musical compositions accurately notated. Study of
these images of musical notation can sometimes prove surprisingly revealing,
as Edward E. Lowinsky shows in his discussion of music associated with St.
Augustine in a painting in the Scuola di San Giorgio degli Schiavoni in Venice.[26]
And Gustave Reese has recently studied a number of such examples in Renaissance intarsia.[27]

Characteristic mythical, philosophical, theological, and educational beliefs
of any age are revealed in scenes which are traditionally depicted with musical
motifs. Representations of music as a liberal art, allegories of hearing as one of
the five senses, and music as one attribute of the various planets, months, and
zodiacal signs all furnish the cultural historian with rich material for research,
as do the many personifications of music or of church modes and the representations of such figures as Tubalcain, King David, Apollo with and without
Marsyas, the Muses, and Orpheus, each shown with his own special musical
iconography.

Sometimes instruments have symbolic meanings when they appear in paintings. Winds may have an erotic significance quite aside from their more literal
relevance to a scene. Patricia Egan has stressed the contrast between the Apol-
lonian lute and the Dionysiac recorder in Giorgione's *Fête champêtre* in the
Louvre.[28] And Hieronymous Bosch's paintings furnish abundant examples of
instruments included, presumably, for symbolic rather than realistic reasons.[29]
On occasion instruments merely identify the role of an individual more precisely: shepherds are traditionally shown with reed pipes, recorders, or bagpipes,
fools with bagpipes, and so on. And some artists painted allegories of music
that attempt to present a more or less systematic survey of all instruments,
or all classes of music.

The musical scholar wishing to use works of art must face the facts that
the success of his research depends on careful assessment of the artistic evidence

26. Edward E. Lowinsky, "Epilogue: The Music in 'St. Jerome's Study,'" *The Art
Bulletin* 41 (1959), 298-301.
27. Gustave Reese, "Musical Compositions in Renaissance Intarsia," in *Medieval and
Renaissance Studies,* ed. John L. Lievsay (Durham, N.C.: Duke University Press, 1968),
pp. 74-97.
28. Patricia Egan, *"Poesia* and the Fête Champêtre," *The Art Bulletin* 41 (1959), 303-
313.
29. See Hans H. Lenneberg, "Bosch's Garden of Earthly Delights, Some Musicological
Considerations and Criticisms," *Gazette des beaux-arts* 58 (September 1961), 135-144.
On symbolism in Bosch's paintings, see Dirk Bax, *Ontcijfering van Jeroen Bosch* (The Hague:
M. Nijhoff, 1949).

and that his questions are as much the province of art history as of music history. The information furnished by a work of art can be believed unreservedly only if the artist's original intentions can be clearly understood and a means of comparing it with other works in the same tradition established. Then a picture is truly worth a thousand words.

Proper evaluation of a large sampling of art works from the same period and place or showing the same subject matter can enable the musical scholar to reach valid conclusions about musical practices. If we were to maintain that no reasoned judgments about musical instruments, performance practice, or cultural history could be made until *all* works of art with musical subjects are gathered and catalogued, we not only would be guilty of a gross exaggeration, but also would have to admit that pictures could probably never be used as musicological evidence. Many are hidden in obscure places or are drifting in the art market. Therefore, we must take care to ask the sorts of questions that available material can help us to answer. Isolated bodies of material that can be controlled bibliographically will yield significant results, but only within limited areas. The best studies to date have almost all confined themselves to investigations of representations of a single subject matter or to the history of a single instrument. It might not be impossible to collect all of the musical subjects in Italian paintings of the Renaissance, for example, using Bernard Berenson's lists as a basic bibliographic control, or in Netherlandish paintings using Max Friedländer's monumental work.[30] A study of musical subjects in French painting at the time of Jean de Berry might be made based on Millard Meiss's fine volumes, and the manuscripts that belonged to the dukes of Burgundy in the fifteenth century might be examined systematically for the information they would furnish about the musical practices of their time.[31] But we must guard against basing conclusions on a restricted number of examples that are not comparable because they come, for example, from different places or times, and we must avoid questions which are too broad to allow us to collect comprehensive samples on which to base research. We must wring as much evidence as we can from pictorial sources, while avoiding as best we can the pitfalls inherent in their use; for with all their drawbacks, they are still our best source of information.

30. E.g., Bernard Berenson, *Italian Pictures of the Renaissance: Florentine School*, 2 vols. (London: Phaidon, 1963); idem, *Central Italian and North Italian Schools*, 3 vols. (London: Phaidon, 1968); and Max Friedländer, *Die altniederländische Malerei*, 14 vols. (Berlin and Leiden: P. Cassirer, 1924-1937), now being revised and translated into English as Max J. Friedländer, *Early Netherlandish Painting*, trans. Heinz Norden, 5 vols. to date (Leiden: A. W. Sijthoff, 1967-).

31. See Millard Meiss, *French Painting in the Time of Jean de Berry: The Late XIV Century and the Patronage of the Duke*, 2 vols. (London: Phaidon, 1967); idem, *The Boucicaut Master* (London: Phaidon, 1968); *La librairie de Philippe le Bon: Exposition organisée à l'occasion du 500e anniversaire de la mort du duc*, ed. Georges Dogaer and Marguerite Debae (Brussels:[Bibliothèque Albert Ier], 1967); and *Le siècle d'or de la miniature flamande: Le mécénat de Philippe le Bon* (Brussels: [Bibliothèque Albert Ier], 1959).

II.
INTRODUCTION

In devising a cataloguing system for the Index of Musical Iconography we have attempted to set up categories that will necessarily focus the user's attention on the ways in which he can assess the value of the individual work of art as evidence. In other words, the system itself takes into account as many aspects of the individual work of art as will conceivably interest the musical scholar. Each object is classified according to its artist, school, date, medium, title, principal subject matter, and the musical evidence it supplies. The classification of many, and perhaps most, objects necessarily involves subjective interpretation. The description of the principal subject matter and musical content of a work of art, for example, cannot issue from a few, simple rules. But the subjective element is kept to a minimum by the formulation of categories that are specific and clearly definable and therefore relatively little susceptible to the vagaries of personal interpretation.

The system is based on a central card which contains all the information gathered about each work divided into categories (see example 1). A series of six cross-reference files separates the categories as follows: (1) school and date, (2) medium or type of object, (3) present location, (4) instruments pictured, (5) subject entries, and (6) bibliography of sources which contain reproductions.

The cross-reference files refer to the central card by locator symbol. The central card file, arranged alphabetically by locator symbol, which is formed of the artists' names or the media and dates of the anonymous works, is, then, the principal source of information. By looking into the various cross-reference files, users can, however, find all of the objects produced during a certain time at a certain place, as well as all of the representations of specific scenes, such as the Nativity, the Tree of Jesse, or Salome's dance, or all depictions of individual instruments (see appendix A for sample cards from the cross-reference files). The criteria for determining the categories form the substance of the following chapters and constitute, in our opinion, the most valuable part of the system, for scholars will not be able to share material efficiently and effectively until they agree on naming the various basic categories of material.

Example 1. The Format of the Main Entry: A Worksheet for the Central Card

Symbol: Repro.:
Artist:
Date/School:
Title:
Medium: Size:
Location:
Description:

Bibl.:

Subjects:

Photographs of all of the items included in the Index, except for those objects illustrated in the books which form a part of our small working library, are stored in separate file cabinets, also arranged according to their locator symbols. Thus, the Index consists of a small working library composed chiefly of reference books and standard anthologies of the history of music in pictures, file cabinets in which separate photographs are stored, and the systems of index cards based on a central file that is arranged by locator symbol.

Although at present all our cross references are typed or written out by hand, the system could in fact be adapted for use by a computer or other advanced technological equipment quickly and easily. Yet no matter how mechanized the gathering and retrieval of widely dispersed material eventually becomes, the most difficult and time consuming part of such a project will always be the process of cataloguing each individual object--deciding on categories of classification and treating all of the works in any one system to a series of systematic procedures. Once scholars agree about the categories of analysis, the specific form which any one index takes is a matter of relatively little importance.

Assembling our own index has convinced us that each scholar or group of scholars will need to have immediate access to some such corpus of material, just as each scholar needs access to a large library. The existence of one, comprehensive, central index would not obviate the need to duplicate work, for each individual scholar would still have to gather and control bibliographically his own personal collection of pictures relevant to his own work. The need for multiple collections does not rule out the possibility or the desirability either of having one central index from which all scholars can draw their collections or of promoting scholarly cooperation. But devising a cataloguing system, or rather a principle of cataloguing, was necessary before questions of cooperation, a central index, or the best way of maintaining an index--manually or by computer--could even be raised. We are confident that scholars can eventually agree on principles of cataloguing and hope that the marvelous diversity of human termperaments will not prevent agreement on any of the other principal questions.

One such question involves the type and quality of reproductions. The core of the Chicago Index consists of pictures of all sizes, shapes, and qualities, from picture postcards and xerographic prints from books to the clearest and most elegant of glossy photographs. The major reason for this diversity is, of course, economy. A wide variety of sources can be gathered relatively inexpensively. Since an index ought principally to be a place where a scholar can find material that will be of use to him, a poor reproduction is better than no reproduction at all. Most bad photographs include enough detail so that a scholar can determine whether or not a better photograph would be useful. The Chicago Index will hopefully lead scholars to more material than they might be able to find casually. But they must evaluate it according to their own needs. The primary concern of a collector should be to gather and cata-

logue as much material as possible, and from a wide variety of sources. Naturally, excellent photographs of every object are desirable—and someday the Chicago
Index may acquire them—but if collections were to be restricted to well-photo-
graphed examples, an index would grow very slowly and be, in the end, less
useful.

The decision to restrict the Chicago Index to Western art before 1800 was
arbitrary and determined chiefly by the need to limit the scope in order to in-
crease the depth of our collection. We chose to eliminate objects made after
1800 because pictorial evidence is more important to research in the performance practices of earlier periods. Collections of wider or differing scope are
equally necessary and useful. Quite aside from their intrinsic interest and value,
studies of musical subjects in Asian and African art, for example, will need to
be made in order to answer many questions about Western medieval musical
practices. But if we have indeed developed a principle of cataloguing as well
as a system that works well within our self-imposed limits, then other users
should have no difficulty in adapting it to non-Western and later art.

III.
FORMING THE LOCATOR SYMBOL

III.1.
Summary of rules

The locator symbol, the brief siglum used to identify a work of art in the cross-reference files and in the central index, is formed of the artist's name (see III.2), or, if the artist is unknown, of the medium and the country and date of origin (see III.3). If the object is a manuscript, the locator symbol is formed of the call number in the library in which it is kept (see III.4). For anonymous book illustrations, the locator symbol is formed of the author's, printer's, or publisher's names, the initials of the title, and the date of publication, or, if the book is anonymous and without printer's or publisher's names, of a shortened version of the title and the date of publication (see III.5).

A simple acquisition number, beginning with one, is added to the substantive part of the locator symbol to differentiate works of the same kind:

> Beham—1: The first work by Sebald Beham catalogued in the Index
> MS Paris BN lat. 9473—4: The fourth illumination from Paris, Bibliothèque
> Nationale, MS lat. 9473 catalogued in the Index
> Painting German 15th c.—8: The eighth anonymous German fifteenth-
> century painting catalogued in the Index
> MachiavelliAW (1580)—1: The first illustration from the 1580 English trans-
> lation of Machiavelli's *Art of Warre* catalogued in the Index
> FleurC—1: The first illustration from *La Fleur des chansons* (n.p., n.d.)
> catalogued in the Index

III.2.
Artist known

III.2.a.

The locator symbol is formed of the artist's family name:

> Cellini: Benvenuto Cellini
> Provost: Jan Provost

III.2.b.

When the family name of a non-Italian artist has a prefix, observe the following rules adapted from *A Manual of Style*, 12th ed. (Chicago: University of Chicago Press, 1969): (1) Keep the prefix if the artist is English (for example, DeQuincy, MacGillivray, Van Buren). (2) Drop the prefix if the artist is German or Dutch (for example, Hoff, van't; Noot, van der). (3) For Spanish, French, and Portuguese artists, keep the prefix if it is an article or a preposition and article forming one word (for example, Del Rio, Du Moncel). If the prefix is a preposition alone or a preposition and article that are separated, drop the preposition but keep the article (for example, La Fontaine, de; Farina, da; Rosny, de).

> Du Cerceau: Jacques du Cerceau
> Eeckhout: Gerbrand van den Eeckhout
> Eyck: Jan van Eyck
> La Hire: Laurent de la Hire
> Le Nain: Antoine Le Nain

III.2.c.

When the given name of an Italian artist is followed by a preposition, or a preposition plus an article (for example, di, da, del, della, dei, degli) followed by a place name or by the artist's father's name, the locator symbol is formed of the artist's given name plus the initial of the other name, and the other name is cross referenced to the symbol. When the given name plus initial is already identified with another artist, use a shortened form of the second name.

> GiovanniM: Giovanni da Milano
> GiovanniP: Giovanni di Paolo
> GiovanniPo: Giovanni dal Ponte
> Milano, Giovanni da. *See* GiovanniM
> Paolo, Giovanni di. *See* GiovanniP
> Ponte, Giovanni dal. *See* GiovanniPo

III.2.d.

When more than one artist have the same second name, add to the locator symbol the initial of the given name in order to differentiate them.

> BelliniG: Gentile Bellini
> BelliniJ: Jacopo Bellini

III.2.e.

When an artist is commonly known by his given name or by a sobriquet, use the more common name for the locator symbol and cross-reference his other name or names.

> Bazzi, Giovantonio. *See* Sodoma
> Bondone, Giotto. *See* Giotto

> Buonarroti, Michelangelo. *See* Michelangelo
> Giotto: Giotto Bondone
> Michelangelo: Michelangelo Buonarroti
> Raphael: Raphael Sanzio
> Sanzio, Raphael. *See* Raphael
> Sodoma: Giovantonio Bazzi, called Il Sodoma

III.2.f.

When two related artists are differentiated from one another by Elder and Younger, form the locator symbol by adding I for the Elder and II for the Younger.

> Bruegel I: Pieter Bruegel the Elder
> Bruegel II: Pieter Bruegel the Younger

III.2.g.

When an artist is known only by his date, his monogram, or the subject or locality of his major work, form the locator symbol of "Mst" plus a short but identifiable form of the descriptive term.

> Mst 1446: Master of 1446
> Mst ES: Master E. S.
> Mst Glorification: Master of the Glorification of the Virgin
> Mst St. Lucy: Master of the St. Lucy Legend

III.2.h.

When a work of art is from an artist's school or shop or is a copy of one of his works, form the locator symbol by adding "school," "shop," or "copy" to his name.

> Giotto copy
> Giotto school
> Giotto shop

III.2.i.

If a work of art is attributed to more than one artist, choose the most reliable or recent attribution as the basis for forming the locator symbol, but cross-reference the rejected artists to the selected one. For example, two paintings in the Borghese Gallery in Rome, one of a singer and the other of a recorder player, are attributed to Giorgione, Giambellino, and Domenico Capriolo. We have accepted the suggestion of Luigi Colletti that the paintings are probably by some provincial follower of Giorgione and have catalogued them "Giorgione school—1 and 2," but we have provided the following cross-references in the central file:

> Capriolo, Domenico. *See also* Giorgione school—1 and 2
> Giambellino. *See also* Giorgione school—1 and 2

III.2.j.

If a work was once attributed to an artist, but the attribution has been withdrawn or denied by most modern scholars, treat the object as an anonymous work, but cross-reference the earlier attribution. In such cases, form the locator symbol according to the rules for anonymous works (see III.3 below). Thus, the so-called *Martelli Mirror* was once attributed to Donatello. We have catalogued it "Utensil Italian 15th c.—1" and provided the following cross-reference in the central file:

Donatello. *See also* Utensil Italian 15th c.—1

III.2.k.

If more than one artist has contributed to a work of art, form the locator symbol from the name of one of them and cross-reference the second to the first. Thus, the *Coronation of the Virgin* by Caterino Veneziano (fl. 1362-1382), and Donato (fl. from ca. 1344; d. before 1398), presently in the Querini- Stampelia Gallery in Venice, is catalogued "VenezianoC—1," but we have provided the following cross reference in the central file:

Donato. *See also* VenezianoC—1

III.2.l.

When a print has been copied from another art work, the locator symbol is formed of the name of the printmaker, who is regarded as the artist, but cross references should be made from the copy to the model and vice versa. For example, Raimondi's engraving of Raphael's *Parnassus* has as its locator symbol "Raimondi—1," but the description of the work includes a reference to "Raphael—1," the locator symbol for Raphael's fresco. Similarly, the description of the fresco refers the user to "Raimondi—1."

III.3.
Artist unknown

III.3.a.

If the artist is not known, form the locator symbol from the medium of the work and its country and century of origin. As the medium of the work, use the capitalized categories in the list of media and types of objects in chapter VIII below. As the country of origin use the capitalized categories in the list of countries and schools in chapter VI below.

Painting Italian 15th c.—1
Print German 16th c.—3
Sculpture French 13th c.—5
Seal Hungarian 11th c.—7

III.3.b.
For rules governing the locator symbols for anonymous sculpture *in situ*, for manuscript illuminations, and for illustrations in printed books, see III.4, III.5, and III.6 below.

III.4.
Sculpture *in situ*

III.4.a.
For all sculpted objects still located on or in the buildings for which they were originally intended or with which they are associated by strong historical ties, form the locator symbol of the word "Sculpture," followed by the name of the city in which the building stands and the initials of the name by which the building is commonly known. For example, the locator symbol "Sculpture Paris ND" refers to an object on or in the Cathedral of Notre Dame, whereas "Sculpture Paris HV" refers to one on or in the City Hall (Hôtel de Ville) in Paris. If the building is a cathedral commonly known only by the name of the city in which it stands, for example, Chartres Cathedral and Exeter Cathedral, omit the initials and form the locator symbol of the word "Sculpture" plus the name of the city only, for example, "Sculpture Chartres" and "Sculpture Exeter." This rule applies to all sculpted altarpieces, architectural sculpture, arms and armor, crosses, fountains and wells, free-standing sculpture, church furniture, secular furniture, commemorative monuments, and sepulchral monuments—in short, to all of those types of objects for which the term "Sculpture" is capitalized in the list in VIII.2.

III.4.b.
Sculpture *in situ* and illuminated manuscripts constitute the only exceptions to the rule that a locator symbol is formed from the artist's name when it is known. Even when the name of a sculptor is known, the locator symbol is formed as described in III.4.a above, and the artist's name is cross-referenced in the central file.

> Antelami, Benedetto. *See* Sculpture Parma B [Parma, Baptistery]

III.5
Manuscript illuminations

III.5.a.
For manuscript illuminations, form the locator symbol of the following elements: the prefix "MS"; the name of the city where the manuscript is located

spelled out in English; the name of the museum, library, or gallery where the manuscript is kept, abbreviated in its native language but still identifiable; the call number of the manuscript; and the usual acquisition number for the Index. If the manuscript has no call number, or if the number is omitted in all of the available reference books, form that part of the locator symbol from the title of the work or from its textual category.

> MS Brussels BR 10.660: Brussels, Bibliothèque Royale, MS 10.660
> MS Cambridge Fitzwilliam 2-1954: Cambridge, Fitzwilliam Museum, MS 2-1954
> MS Hildesheim Godehard St. Albans: Hildesheim, St. Godehards Bibliothek, "St. Albans Psalter"
> MS London BM Cot. Tib. C. VI: London, British Museum, MS Cotton Tiberius C. VI

III.5.b.

Although abbreviations have been avoided as much as possible because they are often very inconvenient to use, certain frequently recurring library names are abbreviated in the locator symbols and in the bibliographical references according to the following scheme:

BM	British Museum, London
BN	Bibliothèque Nationale or Biblioteca Nazionale
BR	Bibliothèque Royale
Cath.	Cathedral Library (in whatever language)
LB	Landesbibliothek
Met	Metropolitan Museum, New York
NG	National Gallery (Galleria Nazionale, and so on)
PL	Public Library
PRO	Public Records Office
SB	Stadtbibliothek or Staatsbibliothek
Univ.	University Library (in whatever language)

III.5.c.

If the present location of a manuscript is unknown, or if it has been destroyed, form the locator symbol by inserting "olim" after the name of the city and library where it was last kept. If that city is unknown, form the locator symbol from the work's author, title, or textual category.

> MS DanteDC I: The first manuscript copy of Dante's *Divine Comedy* catalogued in the Index, for which no present or past location is known
> MS Hours Marguerite B: "Les Heures de Marguerite de Beaujeu," the location of which is not known
> MS Strasbourg Bibl Ville (olim) Hortus: Herrad of Landsberg, "Hortus deliciarum," a manuscript that was in Strasbourg, Bibliothèque de la Ville, until it was destroyed by fire in 1870

III.5.d.

Illuminated manuscripts, along with sculpture *in situ*, are exceptions to the rule that a locator symbol is formed from the artist's name when it is known. Even when the name of the illuminator is known, the locator symbol is formed as described in III.5.a above, and the artist's name is cross-referenced in the central file.

> Pucelle, Jean. *See* MS New York Met 54.1.2

III.6.

Anonymous illustrations in printed books

For anonymous illustrations in printed books, form the locator symbol from the name of the author, publisher, or printer (whichever is known, in that order of precedence), the initials of the title, and, in parentheses, the date of the earliest edition to contain the illustration. If the author's, printer's, and publisher's names are unknown, form the beginning of the locator symbol from a shortened version of the title.

> Agricola(M)MID (1528)—1. The first illustration from Martin Agricola, *Musica Instrumentalis Deudsch* (Wittenberg: Georg Rhaw, 1528) catalogued in the Index (the M in parentheses differentiates Martin from others named Agricola)
>
> AttaingnantLM II (1532)—1: The title page of *Secundus liber tres missas continet* (Paris: Pierre Attaingnant, 1532)
>
> SpenserSC (1597)—1: The first illustration from the 1597 edition of Edmund Spenser's *The Shepherd's Calendar* catalogued in the Index
>
> Basses dances (n.d.)—1: The title page of *S'ensuyvent plusieurs basses dances* (Lyons?: Jacques Moderne? n.d.)

IV.
KIND OF REPRODUCTION AVAILABLE

The kind of reproduction of each work of art on file in the Index is entered under the rubric "Repro." on the first line of the central card (see Example 1, p. 14). The various kinds of reproductions are differentiated by the following code:

B   The work of art is reproduced in a book or article (usually the first work listed in the bibliography) that forms a part of the working library of the Index.
C   The work of art is reproduced as a postcard or greeting card and filed in the photograph file.
F   The work of art is available on microfilm in the Index.
N   A separate negative of the work of art is available in the Index.
P   A separate photograph, either a glossy print or one taken from some ephemeral publication is filed in the photograph file.
S   The work of art is reproduced as a slide, available in the Index.
X   The work of art is reproduced as a xerographic print from a book or article and filed in the photograph file.

A small "c" following any of the above categories signifies that the reproduction in the Index is in color. A small "c" after a bibliographical entry signifies that the reproduction found there is in color. An asterisk preceding an entry in the bibliography signifies that that work is the source of the available reproduction.

V.
ARTIST AND HIS DATES

The rubric "Artist" is filled in with as complete a form of the artist's name as is known, followed by his birth and death dates or as accurate and precise an indication of the period during which he worked as can be discovered. The forms of artists' names and their dates are taken from standard reference works. In cases of doubt, follow Ulrich Thieme and Felix Becker et al., *Allgemeines Lexikon der Bildenden Künstler*, 37 vols. (Leipzig: W. Engelmann, 1907-1950). The pamphlet prepared for the Art Institute of Chicago, G. E. Kaltenbach's *Dictionary of Pronunciation of Artists' Names* (Chicago: Art Institute, 1935), is also a handy reference work for checking artists' names, dates, and schools. We have often accepted as definitive the artist entries in the Max Epstein Archive of The University of Chicago. In any case, where several forms of an artist's name are separated alphabetically, cross-reference the variants to the main entry (thus, "Breughel. *See* Bruegel," but not "Brueghel. *See* Bruegel"). And since the locator symbol is formed of the artist's given name or sobriquet if he is commonly known by one or the other, cross-reference his family name to the main entry (see III.2.e above). See chapter III also for ways of handling conflicting attributions and works of art produced by more than one person.

VI.
SCHOOL AND DATE OF WORK OF ART

VI.1.
Date

The date the work of art was created, as precisely as it is known, should be entered under the rubric "Date/School" on the central card (see Example 1, p. 14). Enter the exact year of creation if it is known; otherwise date the work as closely as possible, for example, "First half [or quarter or third] of the fifteenth century," or merely "Fifteenth century."

Sometimes more than one century will have to be included, for example, "Late fifteenth or early sixteenth century," or even "15th/16th c." Such entries are necessary when an artist's dates overlap two centuries and scholars do not know when in his life a certain work was completed. Thus, the recorder player painted by Giovanni Girolamo Savoldo (1480-1548), reproduced in Frank L. Harrison and Joan Rimmer's *European Musical Instruments* (London: Studio Vista, 1964), no. 99, cannot be dated more precisely than "Late fifteenth or sixteenth century." If an artist is born within the last decade of a century, however, all of his works can safely be dated in the following century. Thus, all works by Francesco Ubertini called Bacchiacca (ca. 1494-1557) can be dated in the sixteenth century, while those by Francesco di Giorgio Martini (1439-1502) must be dated fifteenth or sixteenth century unless more specific information is available.

For a very few works, mostly minor arts from the ancient world, even an approximate date seemed impossible to establish with certainty. For these works, "n.d." should be entered under the rubric "Date/School."

VI.2.
Country or school

VI.2.a.
All countries or schools in which works of art catalogued in the Index originated are listed below in VI.3. We have grouped related countries and attempted to foresee virtually every problem of ambiguity. An object should

be entered in the smallest possible category to which it belongs with certainty. Thus, if a work is unambiguously Flemish, enter it under "Netherlandish: Flemish," but if it is difficult or impossible to know whether the work was produced in Flanders or in Holland, list it as "Netherlandish" without closer identification. A user who wishes to find all Flemish works in the Index, then, must look under "Netherlandish" as well as under "Netherlandish: Flemish." Where a user might be uncertain about the precise meaning of some category, a brief definition of the term is included in the following list. Thus, the term "Early Christian" refers to objects dated between A.D. 1 and A.D. 700 that have Christian subject matter but whose precise country of origin is not known.

VI.2.b.

A separate cross-reference file is kept by school and date so that the user can find all of the objects produced, for example, in Spain in the fifteenth century, or in Bohemia during the thirteenth century, that have been catalogued in the Index.

VI.2.c.

The capitalized portions of countries and schools in the following list are to be used in forming locator symbols for anonymous works (see III.3 above). In forming them it will sometimes be necessary to use two centuries as a date, or even the "n.d." category—for example, "Print German 15th/16th c.";
"Sculpture Hellenistic/Roman n.d."

VI.3.
List of countries and schools

> AEGEAN (ca. 3000-1100B.C.; location not determined more precisely)
> Aegean—CYCLADIC (Aegean [Greek] islands, ca. 3000-1100 B.C.)
> Aegean—HELLADIC (Greek mainland, prehellenic, ca. 3000-1550 B.C.)
> Aegean—MINOAN (Crete, ca. 3000-1400 B.C.)
> Aegean—MYCENAEAN (Greek mainland, prehellenic, ca. 1550-1100 B.C.)
> Albanian. *See* Balkan
> ALSATIAN
> AMERICAN, LATIN
> AMERICAN, NORTH
> Austrian. *See* Germanic—Austrian
> Austro-Hungarian. *See* Germanic—Austrian and Hungarian
> BALKAN (geographically approximate to present-day Albania, Bulgaria, Rumania, European Turkey, and Yugoslavia). For medieval Turkish art *see* Byzantine
> BALTIC (geographically approximate to present-day Estonia, Finland, Latvia, and Lithuania)
> Bohemian. *See* Germanic—Bohemian
> Bulgarian. *See* Balkan
> BYZANTINE (A.D. 320-1453)

Celtic. *See* Insular

Cretan. *See* Aegean—Minoan

Cycladic. *See* Aegean—Cycladic

Czechoslovakian. *See* Germanic—Bohemian

Danish. *See* Scandinavian—Danish

Dutch. *See* Netherlandish—Dutch

EARLY CHRISTIAN (A.D. 1-700. Use only for art work with Christian
  subject whose precise school is not known; if school is known, list by
  school or country.)

ENGLISH. *See also* Insular

Estonian. *See* Baltic

ETRUSCAN (ca. 8th-1st c. B.C.)

Finnish. *See* Baltic

Flemish. *See* Netherlandish—Flemish; Netherlandish—Franco/Flemish;
  Netherlandish—Spanish/Flemish

Franco/Flemish. *See* Netherlandish—Franco/Flemish

FRENCH. *See also* Alsatian; Netherlandish—Franco/Flemish

GERMANIC (includes Tyrolean; location not determined more precisely)

Germanic—Alsatian. *See* Alsatian

Germanic—AUSTRIAN

Germanic—BOHEMIAN

Germanic—GERMAN

Germanic—HUNGARIAN

Germanic—SWISS

Germanic—Tyrolean. *See* Germanic—Austrian; Germanic—Swiss

GREEK (Greek in Greece. For prehellenic art, *see* Aegean—Cycladic, Aegean—
  Helladic, and Aegean—Mycenaean. For Hellenistic art, *see* Hellenistic/Roman)

Greek in Asia Minor

Greek in Balkans

Greek in Greek Islands

Greek in Italy

Greek in Russia

Greek in Sicily

Helladic. *See* Aegean—Helladic

HELLENISTIC/ROMAN (Hellenistic, ca. 323 B.C. to beginning of Christian
  era [A.D.]; Roman, ca. 200 B.C. to ca. A.D. 400; location not determined)

Hellenistic/Roman in Africa

Hellenistic/Roman in Asia Minor

Hellenistic/Roman in Balkans

Hellenistic/Roman in Egypt

Hellenistic/Roman in European countries [by name]

Hellenistic/Roman in Greece

Hellenistic/Roman in Greek Islands

Hellenistic/Roman in Mesopotamia

Hellenistic/Roman in Syria and Palestine

Hungarian. *See* Germanic—Hungarian

ICELANDIC

INSULAR (Irish/Anglo-Saxon, 7th-9th c. A.D.)

IRISH. *See also* Insular

ITALIAN (includes Sicilian; location not determined more precisely). *See
  also* Etruscan

Italian—[region or city]

Latvian. *See* Baltic

Lithuanian. *See* Baltic

Minoan. *See* Aegean—Minoan

Moravian. *See* Germanic—Bohemian

Mozarabic. *See* Spanish

Mycenaean. *See* Aegean—Mycenaean

NETHERLANDISH (location not determined more precisely)

Netherlandish—DUTCH (geographically approximate to present-day Netherlands)

Netherlandish—FLEMISH (geographically approximate to present-day Belgium)

Netherlandish—FRANCO/FLEMISH (Flemish artists working in France)

Netherlandish—SPANISH/FLEMISH (Flemish artists working in Spain)

Norwegian. *See* Scandinavian—Norwegian

POLISH

Portuguese. *See* Spanish; Spanish—Portuguese

Prehellenic. *See* Aegean

PREHISTORIC (Paleolithic, Mesolithic, Neolithic, Bronze, and Iron Ages)

Roman, ca. 200 B.C. to ca. A.D. 400. *See* Hellenistic/Roman

Roman, postclassical. *See* Italian—Roman

Rumanian. *See* Balkan

RUSSIAN (west of Ural Mountains)

SCANDINAVIAN (location not determined more precisely)

Scandinavian—DANISH

Scandinavian—NORWEGIAN

Scandinavian—SWEDISH

SCOTTISH

SPANISH (art of the Iberian Peninsula). *See also* Netherlandish—Spanish/Flemish

Spanish—PORTUGUESE (can definitely be identified as Portuguese, not Spanish)

Swedish. *See* Scandinavian—Swedish

Swiss. *See* Germanic—Swiss

Turkish. *See* Balkan; Byzantine

Tyrolean. *See* Germanic—Austrian; Germanic—Swiss

Yugoslavian. *See* Balkan

VII.
TITLE OF WORK OF ART

VII.1.
Independent object

The title of a work of art is made up of either its commonly known title, written out in English, or a brief description of the subject shown. Whenever possible titles of works of art are taken from the catalogues of the museum, library, or gallery in which the object is kept. In cases where the commonly known title of a work is musically incorrect—where a cittern player is called a lute player, for example—the mistake is corrected without a comment in the Index. In cases where the subject matter is disputed by scholars, the most likely solution has been chosen, and the other suggestions are cross-referenced as subject entries. For example, on the west porch of Chartres Cathedral various sculpted figures personify the seven liberal arts, and beneath each one of them sits an outstanding representative of that discipline. Frank L. Harrison and Joan Rimmer, in *European Musical Instruments* (London: Studio Vista, 1964), no. 48, identify the figure beneath Music as Mathematics, although Emile Mâle, in *The Gothic Image* (New York: Harper Torchbook, 1958), p. 88, more plausibly suggests Pythagoras. The central card in the Index calls the sculpture "Music with Pythagoras," but the suggestion of Harrison and Rimmer is mentioned, and both "Pythagoras" and "Mathematics personified" are included as subject entries.

VII.2.
Manuscripts, books, series, and so on

For manuscript illuminations, illustrations in printed books, and prints published in series, the entry under the rubric "Title" includes basic bibliographical information about the complete work (that is, author, title, publisher, place, and date) as well as the title of the individual part which is being catalogued. Thus, the title of the frontispiece of "The Book of Hours of Catherine of Cleves" is entered as "Book of Hours of Catherine of Cleves—Hours of the Virgin (Matins)—Catherine kneels before the Virgin and Child." The title of a woodcut of a woman playing a harp from Jost Amman's *Kunstbüch-lin* is entered as: "Jost Amman, *Kunstbüchlin* (Frankfurt, Sigmund Feyer-abend, 1599; 4th enlarged ed. of *Kunst und Lehrbüchlein* [1578]), no. 74— Woman playing a harp." And the title of the woodcut from the *Triumph of Maximilian* by Hans Burgkmair and others showing a car filled with lutenists and viol players is entered as: "*The Triumph of Maximilian I*, nos. 17 and 18— Music—Lutes and Viols."

VIII.
MEDIUM OR TYPE OF OBJECT

VIII.1.
Summary of rules

VIII.1.a
The medium of the work of art or the type of object that it is should be determined from the list given below in VIII.2, which includes most media in which Western artists before 1800 worked and most types of objects they created. As the Index expands, however, new categories will have to be added from time to time, especially for the minor arts. A separate cross-reference file by medium and century is kept so that the user can find all the fifteenth-century drawings or seventeenth-century needlework, for example, that are decorated with musical subjects and have been catalogued in the Index. Where categories might prove ambiguous and where their precise limitations might be doubtful, brief definitions or lists of examples have been included in parentheses.

VIII.1.b.
The capitalized parts of the entries in the list are used to form the locator symbols for anonymous works. Thus, the locator symbol for an anonymous roof boss is "Sculpture," although its medium is entered as "Sculpture—Architectural." The locator symbol for an anonymous stove is also "Sculpture," although its medium is entered as "Sculpture—Furniture, secular." The locator symbol for the anonymous decoration on a harpsichord is "Musical instrument," and its medium is entered as "Sculpture—Musical instrument" if the decoration is three-dimensional or as "Painting—Musical instrument" if it is painted. Similarly, the locator symbol for an anonymous bowl is "Utensil," although its medium is entered as "Painting—Utensil" or "Sculpture—Utensil." For anonymous coins, medals, seals, gems, and jewelry, the locator symbol is formed of the one appropriate term—for example, "Coin German 15th c." or "Jewelry Spanish 17th c."—even though they are gathered together in the cross-reference file under "Sculpture—Coins, medals, seals, and stamps" and "Sculpture—Gems and jewelry." For the special way in which sculpture *in situ* is treated, see III.4 above.

VIII.1.c.

An object is listed in the smallest category to which it belongs with certainty, a principle followed throughout the Index. Thus, if the cataloguer is not certain whether a print is a woodcut, an engraving, or an etching, it is entered simply as "Print." But if the print is clearly a woodcut, then it is entered as "Print—Woodcut." In this manner objects can be catalogued even though their exact nature is ambiguous, and the user of the Index can more easily find like objects.

VIII.2.

List of media and types of objects

Altar. *See* Painting—Furniture, church; Sculpture—Furniture, church
Altar canopy. *See* Painting—Furniture, church; Sculpture—Furniture, church
Altarpiece. *See* Painting; Painting—Panel; Sculpture—Altarpiece
Appliqué. *See* Needlework—Appliqué
Aquamanile. *See* Sculpture—Utensil
Archivolt. *See* Sculpture—Architectural
Armor. *See* Sculpture—Arms and armor
Arms. *See* Sculpture—Arms and armor
Basin. *See* Enamel—Utensil; Painting—Utensil; Sculpture—Utensil
Bench. *See* Painting—Furniture; Sculpture—Furniture
BOOK COVER
Book illustration. *See* Manuscript illumination; Print
Boss, roof. *See* Sculpture—Architectural
Bowl. *See* Enamel—Utensil; Painting—Utensil; Sculpture—Utensil
Box. *See* Enamel—Utensil; Painting—Utensil; Sculpture—Utensil
Bracket. *See* Sculpture—Utensil
Cabinet. *See* Painting—Furniture; Sculpture—Furniture
Candelabrum. *See* Painting—Furniture; Sculpture—Furniture
Capital. *See* Sculpture—Architectural
Casket. *See* Enamel—Utensil; Sculpture—Utensil. For Tomb, *see* Sculpture—
    Monument, sepulchral
Cassone. *See* Painting—Furniture, secular; Sculpture—Furniture, secular (N.B.
    A cassone panel is double-listed as Painting—Furniture and as Painting—
    Panel)
Ceiling painting. *See* Painting—Ceiling
Cenotaph. *See* Sculpture—Monument, sepulchral
Censer. *See* Enamel—Utensil, liturgical; Painting—Utensil, liturgical; Sculpture—
    Utensil, liturgical
Ceramic. List under type of object, e.g., Painting—Utensil; Sculpture—Utensil;
    Tile; etc.
Chair. *See* Painting—Furniture; Sculpture—Furniture
Chalice. *See* Enamel—Utensil, liturgical; Painting—Utensil, liturgical; Sculpture—
    Utensil, liturgical
Champlevé. *See* Enamel
Chandelier. *See* Painting—Furniture; Sculpture—Furniture
Chest. *See* Painting—Furniture; Sculpture—Furniture

Choir stall. *See* Painting—Furniture, church; Sculpture—Furniture, church

Ciborium. *See* Enamel—Utensil, liturgical; Painting—Utensil, liturgical; Sculpture—Utensil, liturgical; Sculpture—Furniture, church

Cloissoné. *See* Enamel

Coin. *See* Sculpture—Coins, medals, seals, and stamps

Column. *See* Sculpture—Monument, commemorative; Sculpture—Monument, sepulchral

Console. *See* Sculpture—Architectural

Corbel. *See* Sculpture—Architectural

Cross. *See* Sculpture—Cross

Crown. *See* Sculpture—Gems and Jewelry

Crozier. *See* Enamel—Utensil, liturgical; Painting—Utensil, liturgical; Sculpture—Utensil, liturgical

Cup. *See* Enamel—Utensil; Painting—Utensil; Sculpture—Utensil

Dinanderie (brass and copper ware). List under type of object, e.g., Painting—Utensil; Sculpture—Utensil; etc.

Door (interior and exterior). *See* Marquetry; Painting—Furniture; Sculpture—Architectural; Sculpture—Furniture

DRAWING

Embroidery. *See* Needlework—Embroidery

ENAMEL

ENAMEL—Plaque

ENAMEL—Plaque—Polyptych (i.e., diptych, triptych, or polyptych)

Enamel—UTENSIL (basin, bowl, box, casket, cup, lavabo, plate, etc.)

Enamel—UTENSIL, LITURGICAL (censer, chalice, ciborium, crozier, lavabo, navette, paten, pyx, reliquary, etc.)

Engraving. *See* Print; Print—Engraving; Print—Engraving/etching

Etching. *See* Print; Print—Etching; Print—Engraving/etching

Facade. *See* Sculpture—Architectural

Font. *See* Painting—Furniture, church; Sculpture—Furniture, church

Fountain. *See* Sculpture—Fountains and wells

Frame, mirror or picture. *See* Painting—Furniture; Sculpture—Furniture

Fresco. *See* Painting—Ceiling; Painting—Wall

Furniture. *See* Marquetry; Painting—Furniture; Sculpture—Furniture

Gallery, singing or minstrel. *See* Painting—Furniture, church; Sculpture—Furniture, church

Gargoyle. *See* Sculpture—Architectural

Gate (interior and exterior). *See* Sculpture—Architectural

Gem. *See* Sculpture—Gems and Jewelry

GLASS, STAINED

Glassware. List under type of object, e.g., Painting—Utensil; Sculpture—Utensil; etc. If the object is decorated with enamel or gold, list it as Painting. If it is decorated by an intaglio or relief process (cutting, engraving, etching, etc.), list it as Sculpture.

Hinge. *See* Sculpture—Utensil

Inkwell. *See* Sculpture—Utensil

Intarsia. *See* Marquetry—Intarsia

Ivory. List under type of object, e.g., Book cover; Sculpture—Plaque; Sculpture—Utensil; etc.

Jewelry. *See* Sculpture—Gems and jewelry

Jug. *See* Painting—Utensil; Sculpture—Utensil

Knocker. *See* Sculpture—Utensil

Lace. *See* Needlework—Lace

Lamp. *See* Painting—Utensil; Sculpture—Utensil

Lantern. *See* Painting—Utensil; Sculpture—Utensil

Lavabo. *See* Enamel—Utensil; Enamel—Utensil, liturgical; Painting—Utensil; Painting—Utensil, liturgical; Sculpture—Utensil; Sculpture—Utensil, liturgical

Lectern. *See* Painting—Furniture, church; Sculpture—Furniture, church

Lintel. *See* Sculpture—Architectural

Lithograph. *See* Print—Lithograph

Liturgical object. *See* Enamel—Utensil, liturgical; Painting—Utensil, liturgical; Sculpture—Utensil, liturgical

MANUSCRIPT ILLUMINATION

MARQUETRY

MARQUETRY—Intarsia

Medal. *See* Sculpture—Coins, medals, seals, and stamps

Megolith. *See* Sculpture—Monument, sepulchral

Metalwork. List under type of object, e.g., Enamel—Utensil, liturgical; Painting—Utensil; Sculpture—Utensil, liturgical, etc. If the object is decorated with paint or lacquer, list it as Painting. If it is decorated by an intaglio or relief process (engraving, etching, inlay, niello, repoussé, stamping, etc.), list it as Sculpture. Metalwork decorated with vitreous enamel (glass fused to metal by heat) is listed as Enamel.

Mezzotint. *See* Print—Mezzotint

Mirror case. *See* Sculpture—Utensil

Mirror frame. *See* Painting—Furniture; Sculpture—Furniture

Mold. *See* Sculpture—Utensil

Monstrance. *See* Sculpture—Utensil, liturgical

Monument. *See* Sculpture—Monument, commemorative; Sculpture—Monument, sepulchral

MOSAIC

Musical instrument. *See* Painting—Musical instrument; Sculpture—Musical instrument. For fixed organ, *see* Painting—Furniture, church; Sculpture—Furniture, church

Navette. *See* Enamel—Utensil, liturgical; Painting—Utensil, liturgical; Sculpture—Utensil, liturgical

NEEDLEWORK (not determined more precisely). *See also* Tapestry; Textile

NEEDLEWORK—Appliqué

NEEDLEWORK—Embroidery

NEEDLEWORK—Lace

Obelisk. *See* Sculpture—Monument, commemorative

Organ in fixed position. *See* Painting—Furniture, church; Sculpture—Furniture, church

Organ, movable. *See* Painting—Musical instrument; Sculpture—Musical instrument

PAINTING (not determined more precisely)
PAINTING—Ceiling
PAINTING—Furniture, church (altar, altar canopy, choir stall, font, singing
    or minstrel gallery, lectern, organ in fixed position, pulpit, railing, reredos,
    choir or chapel screen, shrine, tabernacle, throne, etc.)
PAINTING—Furniture, secular (bench, cabinet, candelabrum, cassone, chair,
    chandelier, chest, door, mirror frame, picture frame, stove, table, etc.)
Painting—MUSICAL INSTRUMENT
PAINTING—Panel
PAINTING—Plaque
PAINTING—Tomb
Painting—UTENSIL (basin, bowl, box, cup, lamp, lantern, pitcher, plate, scales,
    urn, vase, etc.)
Painting—UTENSIL, LITURGICAL (censer, chalice, ciborium, crozier, lavabo,
    navette, paten, pax, pyx, reliquary, etc.)
Painting—Vase. *See* Painting—Utensil
PAINTING—Wall
Panel painting. *See* Painting—panel
Paten. *See* Enamel—Utensil, liturgical; Painting—Utensil, liturgical; Sculpture—
    Utensil, liturgical
Pax. *See* Enamel—Utensil, liturgical; Painting—Utensil, liturgical; Sculpture—
    Utensil, liturgical
Picture frame. *See* Painting—Furniture; Sculpture—Furniture
Pitcher. *See* Painting—Utensil; Sculpture—Utensil
Plaque. *See* Enamel—Plaque; Painting—Plaque; Sculpture—Plaque
Plate. *See* Enamel—Utensil; Painting—Utensil; Sculpture—Utensil
PRINT (not determined more precisely)
PRINT—Engraving
PRINT—Engraving/etching (not clear which)
PRINT—Etching
PRINT—Lithograph
PRINT—Mezzotint
PRINT—Woodcut
Pulpit. *See* Painting—Furniture, church; Sculpture—Furniture, church
Pyx. *See* Enamel—Utensil, liturgical; Painting—Utensil, liturgical; Sculpture—
    Utensil, liturgical
Railing. *See* Painting—Furniture; Sculpture—Furniture
Reliquary. *See* Enamel—Utensil, liturgical; Painting—Utensil, liturgical; Sculp-
    ture—Utensil, liturgical
Reredos. *See* Painting—Furniture, church; Sculpture—Furniture, church
Roof boss. *See* Sculpture—Architectural
Sarcophagus. *See* Sculpture—Monument, sepulchral
Screen (choir, chapel, etc.). *See* Painting—Furniture, church; Sculpture—
    Furniture, church
Sculpture. For sculpture still located in or on the building for which it was
    intended, whether or not it is anonymous, *see* the name of the city and
    building where it is [see III.4 above]
SCULPTURE—Altarpiece
SCULPTURE—Architectural (figures attached to and decorating buildings and
    parts of buildings, e.g., archivolt, capital, console, corbel, door, facade,
    gargoyle, gate, lintel, roof boss, trumeau, tympanum, etc.)

SCULPTURE—Arms and armor

Sculpture—COINS, MEDALS, SEALS, and STAMPS (use only one term as locator symbol)

SCULPTURE—Cross (never or no longer part of an altarpiece)

SCULPTURE—Fountains and wells

SCULPTURE—Free-standing (complete in itself, not attached to a building or part of a building, or decorating an object or utensil). *See also* Sculpture—Architectural; Sculpture—Altarpiece; Sculpture—Cross

SCULPTURE—Furniture, church (altar, altar canopy, choir stall, font, singing or minstrel gallery, lectern, organ in a fixed position, pulpit, railing, reredos, choir or chapel screen, shrine, tabernacle, throne, etc.). For moveable organ, *see* Sculpture—Musical instrument; Painting—Musical instrument

SCULPTURE—Furniture, secular (bench, cabinet, candelabrum, cassone, chair, chandelier, chest, mirror frame, picture frame, stove, table, etc.)

Sculpture—GEMS and JEWELRY (use only one term as locator symbol)

Sculpture—Liturgical object. *See* Sculpture—Utensil, liturgical

SCULPTURE—Monument, commemorative (column, obelisk, nonsepulchral stele, shaft, etc.)

SCULPTURE—Monument, sepulchral (cenotaph, column, megalith, sarcophagus, stele, tomb, tombstone, cinerary urn, etc.)

Sculpture—MUSICAL INSTRUMENT (i.e., the decoration on it)

SCULPTURE—Plaque

SCULPTURE—Plaque—Polyptych (small diptych, triptych, or polyptych, not large altarpiece)

Sculpture—UTENSIL (aquamanile, basin, bowl, box, bracket, casket, cup, hinge, inkwell, jug, knocker, lamp, lantern, lavabo, mirror case, mold, pitcher, plate, scale, noncinerary urn, etc.)

Sculpture—UTENSIL, LITURGICAL (censer, chalice, ciborium, crozier [including pastoral staff], lavabo, monstrance, navette, paten, pax, pyx, reliquary, etc.)

Seal. *See* Sculpture—Coins, medals, seals, and stamps

Sepulchral monument. *See* Painting—Tomb; Sculpture—Monument, sepulchral

Shaft. *See* Sculpture—Monument, commemorative

Shrine. *See* Painting—Furniture, church; Sculpture—Furniture, church

Stained glass. *See* Glass, stained

Stamp. *See* Sculpture—Coins, medals, seals, and stamps

Stele. *See* Sculpture—Monument, commemorative; Sculpture—Monument, sepulchral

Stove. *See* Painting—Furniture; Sculpture—Furniture

Tabernacle. *See* Painting—Furniture, church; Sculpture—Furniture, church

Table. *See* Painting—Furniture; Sculpture—Furniture

TAPESTRY. *See also* Needlework; Textile

Terra cotta. List under type of object, e.g., Sculpture

TEXTILE (woven and printed fabrics). *See also* Needlework; Tapestry

Throne. *See* Painting—Furniture, church; Sculpture—Furniture, church

TILE

Tomb. *See* Sculpture—Monument, sepulchral

Tomb painting. *See* Painting—Tomb

Tombstone. *See* Sculpture—Monument, sepulchral

Trumeau. *See* Sculpture—Architectural

Tympanum. *See* Sculpture—Architectural
Urn, cinerary. *See* Sculpture—Monument, sepulchral
Urn, noncinerary. *See* Painting—Utensil; Sculpture—Utensil
Vase painting. *See* Painting—Utensil
Wall painting. *See* Painting—Wall
Watercolor. *See* Painting
Well. *See* Sculpture—Fountains and wells
Woodcarving. List under type of object, e.g., Sculpture—Furniture; Sculpture—Utensil; etc.
Woodcut. *See* Print; Print—Woodcut

IX.
PRESENT LOCATION OF WORK OF ART

The location of the work of art should include the name of the city where
it presently is kept written out in English (plus the country if the city is not
well known); the museum, library, gallery, or whatever spelled out in its native
language; and the acquisition or catalogue number if that is known, or the call
number and page or folio number if the object is a manuscript illumination. If
the present location is unknown, list the last previous location, preceding the
entry with "olim." If no location, past or present, is known, leave the space
blank.

  Thus—New York, Metropolitan Museum, Acq. no. 65.14.1
     Milan, Museo Poldi-Pezzoli, No. 587
     Florence, Santa Maria Novella (Strozzi Chapel)
     Paris, Bibliothèque Nationale, MS fonds fr. 146, fol. 34
     Olim Strasbourg, Bibliothèque de la Ville, MS s. n., fol. 11^{v}

For illustrations in printed books, prints, and all other objects that in their
original form existed in multiple copies, the rubric "Location" can be filled in
by a reference to some bibliographical work that lists all known locations of
all copies. However, if such a work is not available, or does not exist, then list
locations as you find them. The Index does not aspire to list all copies of such
works.

X.
SIZE OF WORK OF ART

When they are known, the overall dimensions of a work of art should be included, preferably as given in a museum or library catalogue, whether that be in inches, centimeters, or millimeters. If the size of the work is not known, leave the space blank.

XI.
BIBLIOGRAPHY: SOURCES WHICH CONTAIN REPRODUCTIONS OR
DISCUSSIONS

Following the rubric "Bibl." on the central card are listed the books and
articles where reproductions or detailed descriptions of the works of art may
be found, or the photograph numbers of one of the various firms which special-
ize in making photographic reproductions of art works. The books are indicated by sigla which normally consist of the author's last name and the first
one or two initials of the work's title. The sigla for museum catalogues and
for catalogues of special exhibitions normally consist of the name of the city
followed by the museum's initials (using the table in III.4.b above, when applicable), the abbreviation "Cat," and the initials of the catalogue's title. All
of these sigla are more completely identified in a separate file.

If the bibliographical reference describes the work but does not include a
reproduction of it, the abbreviation "no ill." is added in parentheses after the
entry. An asterisk precedes those entries from which photographic reproductions have been taken for use in the Index.
Thus:

BerensonIPF	Bernard Berenson, *Italian Pictures of the Renaissance: Florentine School*, 2 vols. (London: Phaidon, 1963).
LeroquaisBM	Victor Leroquais, *Les Bréviaires manuscrits des bibliothèques publiques de France* (Paris: Macon Protat frères, 1934).
WinternitzBL	Emanuel Winternitz, "Bagpipes for the Lord," *The Metropolitan Museum of Art Bulletin* 16 (1958): 276-286.
PalermoNGCat	Raffaello Delogu, *La Galleria nazionale della Sicilia [Palermo]* (Rome: Istituto Poligrafico dello Stato, 1962).
NewYorkMetCatMA	*Medieval Art from Private Collections, A Special Exhibition at the Cloisters, October 30, 1968 through January 5, 1969*, intro. and cat. by Carmen Gómez-Moreno (New York: Metropolitan Museum, 1968).

XII.
DESCRIPTION OF WORK OF ART

XII.1.
Summary of rules

XII.1.a.
The description of the work of art should include the following information: (1) a concise summary of the principal subject matter, including the names of the principal persons; (2) a detailed account of the musical activities and instruments shown, along with some indication of their spatial relationship to the main events; (3) the name of the original owner of the object, or the person who commissioned it and the occasion of its commission if any of these is known; and (4) the text which the work of art illustrates, if such exists and is known. If any text including musical terms or names of instruments accompanies the object, as in many manuscript illuminations and prints, that fact should be noted in the description.

XII.1.b.
The description furnishes material on which the subject entries are based, and these along with the listing of the individual musical instruments represented constitute the most important of the cross-reference files. Thus, the description should be made keeping possible subject entries in mind. Musical instruments should be described following the guidelines set forth in chapter XIV, and musical activities following the guidelines set forth below in XII.4-7.

XII.2.
Examples of descriptions

XII.2.a.
Hard and fast rules can scarcely be made about the amount of detail proper to a description of the principal nonmusical subject matter of a work. Enough detail should be included to enable the user of the Index to understand the context in which the musical activity takes place, and all features of the work

should be described that might possibly have some relevance for musical
scholars. But common sense and some experience with the system will be
better guides than a set of complicated rules. Indeed, a few simple examples,
descriptions of well-known paintings reproduced in the easily accessible volume by H. W. Janson, *History of Art*, rev. ed. (New York, 1969), should make
clear the main principles involved:

XII.2.b.
Masaccio, *Madonna Enthroned* (Janson, *History of Art*, fig. 495): "On either
side of the Virgin and Child are two adoring angels. In front of them are two
angel musicians playing two *lutes.*"
　　This is the simplest type of painting to describe. If two or three saints had
also been shown with the Virgin and Child and they were easily identifiable,
their names should also have been included in the description. St. Barbara and
St. Catherine, for example, are often pictured with the Virgin and Child. But
if there were a large group of people, that is, more than five, surrounding the
central figures, then a simple indication that the group is there and consists
of saints and prophets, or whatever, should suffice. In such cases, both "Saint"
and "Blessed" are entered as subjects. (For a definition of "Blessed," see appendix C.)

XII.2.c.
Pieter Bruegel the Elder, *Peasant Wedding* (Janson, *History of Art*, color pl.
48): "A large group of peasants eat and drink sitting at a long table. They are
attending a wedding banquet, and the bride and groom are present. In front
of the table stand two men playing two *bagpipes* (both with two cylindrical
drones; the single conical chanter of one instrument is also visible)."

XII.2.d.
Jan Vermeer, *The Letter* (Janson, *History of Art*, color pl. 53): "A lady holding a *cittern* (9 strings; frets) is seated in a room in a private house. She seems
to have been interrupted in her playing by a servant bringing a letter. The
central figures are seen through a doorway to a front room. Some of the furniture of the front room is visible, including, in the right foreground, a chair,
on which rest various items, including a single sheet of music; the notes may
be legible."

XII.2.e.
Matthias Grünewald, the *Isenheim Altar* (Janson, *History of Art*, color pl. 46):
"The central panel of the triptych shows the Virgin and Child. On the left
three angel musicians play: (1) a *viol* (7 strings; pegholder not visible; nonrealistic bowing technique); (2) a smaller *viol* (5 strings and pegs; nonrealistic

bowing technique); and (3) a *violin* (3 or 4 strings; pegholder not visible), and a host of angels hover around. Neither the instruments themselves nor the playing techniques of the angels seem musically feasible.

"The left panel depicts the Annunciation, and the right panel the Resurrection."

Thus, the principal subject matter of all panels of a triptych are included (but they are not entered as subjects), even though they have apparently nothing to do with the musical activities, a fact that should be obvious from the description. Moreover, if the musical details are apparently inaccurate or, as here, the artist has painted instruments that could not play, those facts should be noted.

XII.2.f.

Hubert and Jan van Eyck, the *Ghent Altar* (Janson, *History of Art*, fig. 445): "The polyptych consists of two levels, five panels on the lower level, and seven on the upper. The lower level depicts a host of saints, prophets, martyrs, virgins, and so on, coming together to worship the Lamb, who is seen standing on an altar, his blood flowing down through the fountain of life in the center foreground. The adoration of the Lamb symbolizes Christ's sacrificial death.

"On the upper level the outer panels show Adam and Eve, and the three central panels, the Virgin, God, and St. John the Baptist. The remaining two panels (the second and the sixth) depict angel musicians singing and playing instruments.

"In the second panel on the upper level, Eyck portrays eight angels standing around a choirbook and singing. In the sixth panel on the upper level, he paints one angel musician seated at (1) a *positive organ* (21 pipes visible in the front row; one hand stop is seen on the left side of the instrument), and two other angels holding (2) a *nonwaisted fiddle* (5 strings and 3 visible pegs), and (3) a *frame harp* (ca. 24 strings). Two more angels, apparently not musical, are visible in the background."

XIII.
SUBJECT ENTRIES

XIII.1.
Main subject matter

XIII.1.a.
Importance of subject entries and cross references

The subject-entry file groups together works of art in like categories; under each category individual works are listed by locator symbol. Thus, the subject entry file and the musical instruments file are the heart of the Index, for here the scholar will find assembled in convenient form the raw material for his research. The following kinds of information are collected for each art work: the main subject matter, the principal persons, the type of book or manuscript, the number and kinds of musical performers, the type of musical activity, musical equipment, the location and occasion of the musical activity, and the names of instruments, musicians, or musical terms found in texts accompanying the work of art. All subject entries gathered to date in the Index of Musical Iconography are listed alphabetically in appendix C. The present chapter explains the principles followed in assembling that list.

Clear, self-explanatory terms are required to describe the main subject matter of a work—terms which are narrowly enough conceived to avoid excessive overlapping and yet broad enough to encompass the variations in detail with which artists of various periods have treated the same subject. In most cases, a mythological, historical, allegorical, or religious scene can be summarized in more than one way. Thus, "Virgin and Child" might as easily be called "Madonna and Child" or "Mary and Christ," and paintings depicting Salome dancing before Herod might be called "Salome's dance," or "The Feast of Herod," or "Herod's Feast." To avoid confusion about terminology, we have copiously cross-referenced each of the terms describing a particular scene. Thus, the Adoration of the Shepherds, for example, is filed under "Christ—Adoration of the Shepherds," and cross references under "Adoration," "Shepherds," and "Virgin" send the user to the correct main entry. Entries under "Madonna," "Mary," and "St. Mary" instruct the reader to consult "Virgin," the term adopted as the central one. Pictures of the Flight into Egypt, filed under "Christ—Flight into Egypt," are cross-referenced from "Flight," "Egypt," "Virgin," and "St. Joseph." Although these cross references may seem extravagant and unwieldy, they have helped to avoid duplication in forming the Index, and they should assist the reader to find the material he wishes more easily. Even if an incorrect term is entered on the central card, as occasionally happens with such a complex system, cross references will steer the cataloguer to the correct entry.

XIII.1.b.
Main subject matter described by other categories

Quite often the main subject matter may be described in naming the principal persons, in identifying the occasion for the musical activity, or even in enumerating the number of performers. Thus, Tristan and Isolde, Apollo and Marsyas, or Orpheus and Eurydice are apt to be the main subject matter of works of art in which they are the principal persons. The terms "Guild celebration" and "Theatrical spectacle with music" might well explain the chief thing represented as well as the occasion for the musical activity. A portrait of an anonymous lutenist can be said to depict a "Solo musician," a term that encompasses the principal subject matter as well as the number of performers. Categories like "Still life, musical," which function solely as a description of the subject matter, are relatively rare.

XIII.1.c.
Sobriquets and series titles

If a work of art is commonly known by some sobriquet, it, too, should be listed as a subject entry so that the work may more easily be found in the Index. Thus, "Ghent Altar," "Cluny capitals," "Donne Triptych," "Eadwine Psalter," and "Hours of Jeanne d'Evreux" are all entered in the cross-reference file.

Similarly, if a painting or print is one of a series, the name of the entire series should be listed as a subject entry, for example, "Hochzeitstänzer," "Triumph of Maximilian I," or "Dance of Death." Sometimes a series title will also indicate the main subject matter, for example, when music is depicted as one of the seven liberal arts ("Liberal arts—Music") or as one of the five senses ("Senses, allegory of—Hearing").

XIII.1.d.
List of sacred scenes with music

Music appears again and again in a relatively small number of sacred scenes in western art. Some of the most frequently found sacred subjects and Biblical characters associated with music are listed below for convenience of reference. These are incorporated into appendix C, the list of subject entries gathered to date.

Absalom
Adam and Eve
Ahasuerus, feast of (Book of Esther)
Apocalypse. *See* Text—Bible—Revelation; Text—Bible—Biblical adaptation.
    See also names of individual apocalypses.
Apocalypse, Elders of
Blessed (groups of saints, martyrs, virgins, patriarchs, prophets, confessors,
    apostles, etc. found in scenes depicting heaven by whatever name, e.g.,
    the City of God, the New Jerusalem, etc.). *See also* David and Blessed;
    Last Judgment
Christ. *See also* Last Judgment; Trinity; various subentries under Virgin
Christ—Adoration of the Magi. *See also* Epiphany
Christ—Adoration of the Shepherds
Christ—Among Doctors
Christ—Ascension
Christ—Baptism
Christ—Bearing Cross
Christ—Before Pilate
Christ—Betrayed
Christ, birth of. *See* Christ—Nativity
Christ—Blessing. *See* Christ
Christ Child. *See* St. Christopher; Virgin and Child; Virgin and Child—In
    garden
Christ—Crucifixion
Christ enthroned. *See* Christ
Christ—Entombment
Christ—Flagellation
Christ—Flight into Egypt
Christ—Harrowing of Hell
Christ—Holy Women at Sepulchre
Christ—In Mandorla. *See* Christ
Christ—Miracles
Christ—Miracles—Cana
Christ—Miracles—Raising Lazarus
Christ—Mocking
Christ—Nativity. *See also* Christ—Adoration of the Magi; Christ—Adoration of
    the Shepherds
Christ—Preaching
Christ—Presentation in the Temple
Christ—Resurrection
Christ—Temptation
City of God. *See* Angel musician; Angel musician, wingless; Blessed
Creation. *See also* Adam and Eve
David alone
David and Bathsheba
David and Blessed
David and Goliath
David and musicians
David and Samuel
David and Saul
David anointed king. *See* David and Samuel
David as psalmist. *See also* David alone; David and musicians

David as shepherd
David greeted by Israelites. *See* David, Triumph of
David in Jesse Tree. *See* Jesse Tree
David—Return of the Ark
David, Triumph of (1 Sam. 18:6)
Epiphany. *See also* Christ—Adoration of the Magi
God the Father. *See also* Creation
Golden Calf, worship of. *See* Ceremony, religious—Pagan—Worship of Golden
      Golden Calf
Good Shepherd. *See* David as shepherd; Orpheus as shepherd; Shepherd
Heaven. *See* Angel musician; Angel musician, wingless; Blessed; Putto musician;
      Putto musician, winged
Hell
Herod
Herod, feast of
Herod—Massacre of the Innocents. *See* Massacre of the Innocents
Holy Spirit, Dove of
Jericho, Battle of
Jesse Tree
Jonah and the whale
Last Judgment
Massacre of the Innocents
Nebuchadnezzar, idol of
Paradise. *See* Angel musician; Angel musician, wingless; Blessed; Putto musi-
      cian; Putto musician, winged; Virgin—Assumption; etc.
Popes. *See* names of individual popes
Prodigal Son
Red Sea, crossing of
Saints. *See* names of individual saints
Salome. *See* Herod, feast of
Samson and Philistines
Shepherds, Annunciation to
Solomon
Solomon and Queen of Sheba
Solomon, court of
Solomon, judgment of
Trinity
Virgin. *See also* various subentries under Christ
Virgin and Child
Virgin and Child—In garden
Virgin—Annunciation
Virgin—Assumption
Virgin—Coronation
Virgin—Death
Virgin enthroned. *See* Virgin and Child
Virgin in garden. *See* Virgin and Child—In garden
Virgin—Miracles
Virgin—Seven Joys
Virgin—Visitation

XIII.1.e.

Music itself as principal subject matter

Music itself is sometimes the main subject matter of a work of art. For convenience of reference the main categories into which such works will fit are listed below:

> Instrumentarium, complete (a more or less systematic survey of all musical instruments, or at least of all categories of instruments). *See also* Angel musician
> Liberal arts—Music
> Mode, church, personified
> Muses
> Music as a worldly pleasure (scenes illustrating the concept of worldly, sinful, or illicit pleasures by means of musical subjects; implied is some contrast with spiritual pleasures or condemnation of secular music-making)
> Music personified
> Music personified with stag
> Musica mundana, humana, instrumentalis
> Senses, allegory of—Hearing

XIII.2.
Principal persons

XIII.2.a

Proper names as subject entries

The following proper names should be listed as subject entries: (1) the names of the principal persons shown in the work of art, whether historical, mythological, Biblical, or allegorical, and whether or not they are actually taking part in the musical activities; (2) the name of the original owner of the object or the person who commissioned it if either is known; (3) if the object is an illustration in a printed book, the names of the author, printer, and publisher if they are known; (4) if the object is a manuscript, the name of the author of the text if it is known; and (5) if the scene depicts musicians employed by one man, for example, a king or a prince, his name. Thus, a name appearing in the subject entry file indicates that the work of art portrays that person, or the musicians employed by him, or reflects in one way or another the music connected with him.

XIII.2.b.

Greek and Roman names

Certain figures of antiquity, chiefly gods, goddesses, and heroes, have both a Greek and a Roman name. They are listed by a composite, the Greek name preceding the Roman, for example, Eros/Cupid, Odysseus/Ulysses, Hermes/Mercury. The second name is cross-referenced to the main entry.

XIII.2.c.
Omitting proper names

In certain cases names of people actually portrayed are omitted. Some scenes imply the presence of a stock cast of characters. The angel Gabriel, for example, is always present at the Annunciation, even though the main subject entry "Virgin—Annunciation" does not list him. Similarly, Joseph and Mary are always shown in the Flight into Egypt, but the main subject entry for that scene is "Christ—Flight into Egypt." In most such cases, cross references obviate the necessity of repeating these names each time they reappear. Thus, the entry "Gabriel" refers the reader to "Virgin—Annunciation." Moreover, in scenes showing many minor characters, each might be identified by name, but little would be gained by doing so, and therefore they are ignored. In some cases, groups are identified by class, for example, "Saints." The term "Blessed" is used to describe those large groups of people often shown in sacred scenes, the saints, apostles, prophets, martyrs, and so on who gather to worship the Lamb in the *Ghent Altarpiece*, who make up the heavenly host in Resurrections, Assumptions, Ascensions, and Coronations of the Virgin, or who sometimes surround the Virgin and Child. Normally, more than five people are considered a group too large to be more closely identified. In cases of doubt, it should be remembered that only the persons taking part in the main activity of a scene need be listed by name or class. Thus, nonmusical angels are not listed, nor are nonmusical animals shown in the margins of manuscripts.

XIII.3.
Printed books and manuscripts

XIII.3.a.
Summary of rules

In cataloguing an illustration in a printed book or an illumination in a manuscript, the following information should be included, each listed as a subject entry: (1) the author of the work and, if it is printed, the publisher and/or printer; (2) the title of the work if it is anonymous or if it is a literary text; (3) the type of text, described according to the categories enumerated in XIII.3.c. below; (4) whether the illustration is a title page (entered as "Title page") or a marginal decoration or bas-de-page (entered as "Marginal ornament, musical"); (5) the subject of the main miniature if the illustration is marginal; and (6) references to music in the accompanying text. The description of such illustrations should also normally include some reference to the specific passage of the text which is being illustrated.

XIII.3.b.
Marginal ornaments

Whether or not marginal ornaments relate thematically to the main miniature is a question art historians still frequently debate. Therefore, the subject of the main miniature needs to be listed as a subject entry as well as the subject of the marginal ornament. Thus, one page of the "Hours of Jeanne d'Evreux" shows the Nativity as the main miniature and a bas-de-page with shepherds playing musical instruments; the subject entries are listed as "Christ—Nativity," "Shepherd musician," and "Marginal ornament, musical."

XIII.3.c.
Categories of texts

Knowing the type of text from which an illustration comes may help the musical scholar to isolate groups of pictures with musical subjects which are related thematically. The following categories have been devised; they seem to be flexible enough to encompass all the texts illustrated with musical subjects thus far encountered. As with every other category in the Index, texts are placed in the smallest one to which they belong with certainty. Thus, if the cataloguer knows that the text is literary, but is unsure of its contents, it is entered as a "Text, literary" rather than in one of the subcategories. The list below is merely an outline. As the Index grows, more categories will be added following the pattern already established.

XIII.3.d.
List of categories of texts

> Musical source illustrated (illustrations in manuscripts and printed collections of music). *See also* Text, liturgical
> Text—Bible (complete Bibles, separate Old Testaments, separate New Testaments, Bible commentaries and parts thereof)
> Text—Bible—Acts
>> 1 Chronicles
>> Esther
>> Exodus
>> etc.
>> Psalms. Illustrations known to be from the Book of Psalms, but whose specific psalm number is not known. The number of the specific psalm illustrated is entered when known. *See also* Text: Psalter, which includes all psalter illustrations, not just those illustrating the psalms.
>> Psalm 1
>> Psalm 19 (King James, 20)
>> Psalm 21 (King James 22)
>> etc.
> Text—Biblical adaptation (includes the Bible historiale, Biblia pauperum, Bible moralisée, versifications of the complete Bible, versifications of parts of the Bible, etc.)

Text—Description of festival
Text, didactic—Astronomy and astrology
      Calendar (illustrations from sources that are only calendars, not calendars that are parts of larger works). *See also* Months, music associated with (which includes illustrations from various sources such as books of hours, psalters, etc.)
      Chess
      Dance
      Encyclopedia
      Exemplum (short tales or poems offering moral instruction by example)
      Feminist
      Fine Arts
      Grammar
      Hunting
      Military
      Music
      Natural history
      Natural history—Bestiary
      Topography
      Travel and social customs
Text—Haggadah
Text, hagiographic
Text, historical—Archival records
      Biography
      Chronicle
Text—Hours
Text—Hours—Office of St. Louis
Text, legal—Decretals
      Guild statutes
      Patents of nobility
Text, literary. (List as a subject entry the title of every work analyzed as a literary text, whether the author is known or not. Thus, the subject entries for illustrations from the *Divine Comedy* include "Dante—Divina Commedia," as well as "Text, literary—Romance or epic." The only exception to this rule involves complete or collected works, the titles of which are not listed separately.)
Text, literary—Drama
      Lyric poetry
      Romance or epic (including *chansons de gestes*)
      Short tales. *See also* Text, didactic—Exemplum
Text, liturgical—Antiphonary
      Breviary
      Diurnal
      Gradual
      Lectionary
      Missal
      Ordinal
      Passional
      Pontifical
      Troper

Text, philosophical or theological
Text—Psalter

XIII.3.e.
Names for musical instruments given in work of art or accompanying text

When a text accompanying a manuscript illumination, an illustration in a printed book, an isolated print, or any other work of art mentions musical instruments, musical terms, or musicians, those are listed as subject entries. In most cases, the musical instruments mentioned in an accompanying text will presumably be the ones illustrated, but sometimes an artist actually labels an instrument with its proper name. Whichever alternative the artist chose, the subject entry should read "Instrument, reference to—[Instrument name]." Most instruments are named in foreign languages. To preserve the original as closely as possible, keep the grammatical case in which the instrument is mentioned, for example, "Instrument, reference to—Tympanorum."

XIII.3.f.
Musical terms given in work of art or accompanying text

Musical terms mentioned in an accompanying text should be listed as subject entries in the grammatical case in which they occur. The notation "[lit]" following a term indicates that the word is mentioned in the text but not specifically illustrated by the picture. For examples, see "Musical term" in appendix C.

XIII.3.g.
Names for musicians given in work of art or accompanying text

If types of musicians, for example, "Cantatores," "Reichstrumeter," or "Ribeber," are mentioned in the work of art or in the text accompanying it, those terms should be listed as subject entries in the grammatical case in which they occur. All such terms are gathered together in Appendix C under "Musician, reference to."

XIII.4.
Number and kind of performers

XIII.4.a.
Number

The total number of performers shown in a picture is listed as a subject entry, using the following scheme: solo musician, duet, trio, quartet, quintet, and sextet or larger ensemble. In many cases, a picture will seem to depict more than one group of performers. If there is good reason to suppose that two or more separate ensembles of musicians are playing, enter the number of each possible combination in addition to the total number. Thus, in the *Ghent Altar* (Janson, *History of Art*, fig. 445), the eight singing angels are separated from the three angels holding instruments; therefore "Trio" is listed as a subject entry in addition to "Sextet or larger ensemble." When there is no doubt at all that various groups of musicians are playing separately, the total number of performers need not be listed.

When the number of performers is not clear, because, for example, some may or may not be singing, list as subject entries all of the probable groupings. The miniature at the beginning of a fifteenth-century "Romance of the Rose" in the British Museum (MS Harley 4425, fol. 12, reproduced in Lesure, *Musik und Gesellschaft im Bild* [Cassel: Bärerretter, 1966], pl. 5), for example, includes a lutenist and either two or three singers. Both "Trio" and "Quartet" should be listed as subject entries.

XIII.4.b.
Type and social position

If the performers are human, their social position or general type as well as their names should be listed as subject entries, if one or both facts are known. The list given in XIII.4.d. below can serve as a guide in determining the kinds of possible performers. It is not always possible to categorize musicians in this way, and so sometimes this category must be omitted.

XIII.4.c.
Genus of nonhuman performers

If the performers are not human, their genus, for example, angel, animal, or grotesque, should be listed as subject entry if their names are not known.

XIII.4.d.
List of types of performers

The following list of types of musicians is not comprehensive, but comprises the categories now in use in the Index of Musical Iconography. For a list of names applied to various types of musicians in pictorial sources before 1800, see "Musician, reference to" in appendix C.

> Acrobat or juggler musician
> Actor musician. *See also* Komast; Theatrical spectacle with music
> Amateur musician. *See* Informal music-making
> Angel musician. *See also* Putto musician; Putto musician, winged
> Angel musician, wingless
> Animal musician
> Animal musician—Ape
>   Bear
>   Cat
>   Donkey
>   etc.
> Bacchante musician

Beggar. *See* Street musician

Bourgeois music. *See* Informal music-making

Centaur musician (half man, half horse; walks on four legs). *See also* Satyr
musician

Cleric playing instrument

Cleric singing. *See also* Singing, sacred; Singing, secular

Court musician. *See* Court, music at

Devil musician

Dwarf musician

Fool or jester musician

Genius. *See* Angel musician; Angel musician, wingless; Poet as creator; Putto
musician; Putto musician, winged

God, river, musician

God, sea, musician

Grotesque musician (partly human and partly animal)

Herald. *See* Announcement, public, with music

Humanist musician (a single musician playing lute or lira da braccio or singing
to a group either in a room [often a classroom] or gathered around him
in a city street; when indoors there is often a podium at which he stands
or sits)

Jewish musician. *See* Jewish music

Jongleur (professional instrumentalist playing in a noncourtly milieu. When
jongleurs play at courts, they are listed under "Court, music at"). *See also*
Acrobat or juggler; Acrobat or juggler musician; Civic music; Court, music
at; Street musician. For jongleur after 1400, *see* Minstrel

Juggler. *See* Acrobat or juggler

Komast (an actor in a comedy in ancient times, usually holding a musical instrument or phallic symbol, sometimes masked, found primarily on Greek
vases)

Landsknecht. *See* Military subjects

Maenad musician. *See* Bacchante musician

Meistersinger

Middle-class music. *See* Informal music-making

Minnesinger. *See* Court, music at—Minnesinger

Minstrel (a professional instrumentalist who belonged to a guild; minstrels
functioned as court musicians, town musicians, and sometimes as street
musicians and also accompanied church choirs). *See also* Civic music;
Court, music at; Singing, sacred—With instruments; Street musician. For
minstrels before 1400, *see* Jongleur

Monster musician. *See* Grotesque musician

Mummer. *See* Masquerade

Musical couple (a man and woman, one or both of whom is making music;
more than one musical couple is also included in this category)

Mythological figure, anonymous, musician

Nereid musician. *See* Nymph musician

Nymph musician (includes water nymphs [Naiads and Nereids], wood nymphs
[Dryads], and mountain and grotto nymphs [Oreads]). *See also* Bacchante
musician

Peasant. *See* Rustic music

Pilgrim musician

Priest or priestess. *See* Ceremony, religious—Judaeo-Christian; Ceremony, religious—Pagan; Cleric playing instrument; Cleric singing

Putto musician (young, childlike spirits of the Cupid or cherub class, with or without wings, who function as angels in Christian art; they descended from the Graeco-Roman Erotes or Cupids to become the Amorini or putti of Renaissance art). *See also* Angel musician; Angel musician, wingless; Music stand—Putto holding music

Putto musician, wingless

Sailor. *See* Ship, music in

Satyr musician (Includes silenus and faun musicians. Satyrs were goat-men like Pan. Sileni were part man and part horse, walked on two legs, not four; often had horses' hooves instead of feet, sometimes horses' ears, and always horses' tails. Fauns were Roman satyrs.) *See also* Centaur musician

Shepherd musician. *See also* Christ—Adoration of the Shepherds; David as shepherd; Orpheus as shepherd; Shepherds, Annunciation to

Silenus musician. *See* Satyr musician

Siren musician

Skeleton. *See* Dance of Death; Memento mori

Soldier. *See* Military subjects

Stadtpfeifer. *See* Civic music

Street musician (beggars or poor itinerant musicians). *See also* Acrobat or juggler; Minstrel; Serenade

Student musician (a student playing music, not to be confused with a music student)

Town musician. *See* Civic music

Triton musician

Troubadour. *See* Court, music at

Trouvère. *See* Court, music at

Warrior. *See* Military subjects

XIII.5.
Kinds of musical activity

XIII.5.a.
Summary of rules

Purely instrumental performances are adequately catalogued by listing the musical instruments and the number and kinds of performers. But the kinds of musical activities that do not involve playing instruments, that is, singing, dancing, teaching, conducting, and instrument making, need also to be listed as subject entries.

XIII.5.b.
Singers and singing

When the work of art shows people singing, first determine whether they are apt to be singing pagan, secular, or sacred music (listed as "Singing, pagan," "Singing, sacred," or "Singing, secular"). Usually the context will leave little doubt about the correct decision; if the work is ambiguous in this respect, list the subject entry merely as "Singing." If instruments play with the singer or singers, add the phrase "with instruments" to the subject entry, for example, "Singing, secular—With instruments."

If only one person is singing, whether entirely alone and without accompaniment or with one or more instruments, a second subject entry ("Singing, solo") should indicate that fact. Thus, two subject entries dealing with singing can be listed for a single picture. A painting of a solo lutenist who seems to be singing to his own accompaniment, for example, would be catalogued under "Singing, secular (or sacred)—With instruments," and "Singing, solo," in addition to "Solo musician."

XIII.5.c.
Dancers and dancing

When the work of art shows people dancing, first determine whether they are performing couple, religious, round, solo, or theatrical dances (listed as "Dancing, couple," "Dancing, round," and so on). If horses are shown dancing, list as subject entry "Dancing—Horse ballet."

If the context or the accompanying text makes clear that the performers are executing a specific dance step, that fact should also be indicated, for example, "Dancing—Basse dance," "Dancing—Volte," and so on.

If the name of the dance tune is included in the picture or identified in the accompanying text, it, too, should be listed under the specific step, for example, "Dancing—Pavane—'Belle qui tiens ma vie.'"

XIII.5.d.
Teachers of music

If a teacher is shown with one or more pupils, the subject entry "Instruction, musical" should be listed, which thus may indicate a private lesson, a classroom lecture, or a singing school.

XIII.5.e.
Conductors

If one person seems to be conducting, or even beating time to the music, list as subject entry "Conducting" or "Conducting—Baton."

XIII.5.f.
Instrument makers

If a picture shows a person making instruments, or a shop where they might be made, list as subject entry "Instrument making." If the picture shows a specific instrument being made, list the instrument following the main entry, for example, "Instrument making—Bell."

XIII.6.
Musical equipment

XIII.6.a.
Summary of rules

Printed and manuscript music, instrument cases, music stands, charts and diagrams, and other musical accessories should be listed as subject entries when they appear in a picture. The genres and titles of compositions illustrated should be listed when they are known. Theatrical stage settings and costumes should also be catalogued.

XIII.6.b.
Describing a work of art which pictures a piece of music

List printed and manuscript music according to whether it is a choirbook, a music book, or a music sheet. A choirbook is a large volume that rests on a stand around which people gather to perform. A music sheet is any unbound page, scroll, or roll with musical notes. A music book is a bound volume that is smaller than a choirbook—generally such a volume is held in the hand or rests on a table. During the Renaissance, most music books were either part books or small volumes in so-called choirbook format.

If the musical notation is legible, or there is reason to believe that the music can be read from the original work of art, even though the reproduction is not good enough to make it out, list as a subject entry "Musical notation."

XIII.6.c.
Genre and title of composition illustrated

If the artist has made clear the genre of the composition that the musicians are performing, list it as a subject entry. If the title of a composition is included in the picture or the accompanying text identifies it, list it under the genre as a subject entry, for example, "Chanson—'J'ay pris amours.'" The following list of genres comprises the principal entries gathered to date. As the Index grows, more categories will be added, following the pattern already established.

> Canon
> Cantata
> Canzona
> Carmen—Italian text
>   Textless
> Chanson
> Dances. [See XIII.5.b.]
> Hymn
> Lauda
> Lied
> Madrigal
> Mass and Office. *See also* Hymn.

Mass and Office—Antiphon
Antiphon, Marian
Gloria
Introit
Invitatory
Kyrie
etc.
Motet
Opera
Ricercare

XIII.6.d.
Instrument cases, music stands, and so on

List instrument cases, music stands, foot rests, tuning keys, bands or thongs for holding instruments (entered as "Instrument support"), and other musical accessories as subject entries. When possible, include the name of the instrument for which the case was intended, for example, "Instrument case—Lute," "Instrument case—Flute/recorder," and so on. Since choirbooks are assumed to rest on stands, it is not necessary to list "Music stand" as a subject entry each time a choirbook appears in a picture.

XIII.6.e.
Charts and diagrams

When charts and diagrams appear in a picture, list them as subject entries under whatever category seems most appropriate, for example, "Fingering chart," "Guidonian hand," "Solmisation syllables," and so on.

XIII.6.f.
Theatrical stage settings and costumes

When theatrical stage settings or people in theatrical costumes appear in a picture, they should be listed as "Theater—Costume design," or "Theater—Stage setting." Pictures of costumes and stage settings, along with portraits of composers and other musicians, are virtually the only items catalogued in the Index which do not actually show some type of musical activity. If the title of the ballet, intermedio, opera, or other theatrical entertainment for which the costumes or stage settings were prepared is known, it, too, should be listed as a subject entry, along with the name of the composer (of ballets and operas) or poet (of *intermedii*). The following examples will clarify the division of the subject matter:

Carrousel
Douairière de Billebahaut, La. See Theater—Costume design—Ballet—*Douairière de Billebahaut;* Theater—Stage setting—Ballet—*Douairière de Billebahaut*
Incoronazione di Poppea, L'. See Opera—*Incoronazione di Poppea* (Monteverdi)

Intermedio—*Pellegrina, La* (Girolamo Bargagli)
Pellegrina, La. See Intermedio—*Pellegrina, La* (Girolamo Bargagli)
Theater—Costume design—Ballet—*Douairière de Billebahaut, La*
Theater—Costume design—Intermedio
Theater—Costume design—Opera
Theater—Stage setting—Ballet—*Douairière de Billebahaut, La*
Theater—Stage setting—Commedia dell'arte
Theater—Stage setting—Intermedio. *See* Intermedio
Theater—Stage setting—Opera. *See* Opera
Theatrical spectacle with music. *See also* Carrousel; Dancing, theatrical;
   Intermedio; Opera; Theater—Costume design; Theater—Stage setting

XIII.7.
Location and occasion of musical activity

XIII.7.a.
Summary of rules

The following information about the location and the occasion of the musical activity should be supplied for each picture catalogued: (1) the name of the city and the building or section of the city where the music is being played, if known; (2) if the musicians are performing in any of the special playing positions listed in XIII.7.c. below, that fact should be noted; and (3) if the performance is taking place in any of the locations or for any of the occasions listed in XIII.7.d. below, that fact should be noted. For some works of art, no location or occaion can be specified, or the occasion is implied by the main subject matter. The subject entry "Virgin and Child," for example, satisfactorily explains the occasion for performance of angel musicians. And, indeed, angel musicians are seldom listed as playing for a specific occasion or in a specific location.

XIII.7.b.
City where performance takes place

List the name of the city, followed by the building or section of the city where the music is being performed, if any of that information is available, for example, "Florence," "Florence—Palazzo Vecchio," "Florence—Piazza Santa Croce," and so on.

XIII.7.c.
Special locations where musicians often are found

If the musicians are performing in any of the special locations listed below, that fact should be noted:

Car or float, musician on
Gallery, musicians'

> Musician, mounted (on a real animal, not a grotesque creature, bird, fish, etc.)
> Pedestal, musician on
> Pit, musicians'
> Platform, musician on
> Tower, arch, gate, wall, etc., musician on

XIII.7.d.
List of locations and occasions gathered to date

The following list of locations and occasions is not comprehensive, but comprises the categories now in use in the Index of Musical Iconography. Where terms are used with special meanings or are in themselves ambiguous, brief definitions are given in parentheses:

> Academy, music at (musical scene at sixteenth- or seventeenth-century academy, chiefly Italian; usually musicians are shown singing or playing around a table on which no food or drink is visible). *See also* Meistersinger
> Announcement, public, with music
> Artist and music (a musical subject in an artist's studio)
> Athletic event, music at
> Bacchanal. *See* Ceremony, religious—Pagan
> Ball. *See* Dancing, couple
> Ballet. *See* Dancing, theatrical; Theater—Costume design—Ballet; Theater—Stage setting—Ballet
> Balletto de cavallo. *See* Dancing—Horse ballet
> Banquet. *See* Meal, music at
> Bath, music in
> Bourgeois music. *See* Informal music-making
> Canonical hours. *See* Ceremony, religious—Judaeo-Christian
> Ceremony, religious—Judaeo-Christian
>   Pagan
> Chess game, music at
> Church, music directly outside
> Church, music inside
> Civic music
> Contest, musical
> Coronation
> Country fair. *See* Rustic music
> Court, music at (music performed by or for rulers or their courtiers; the picture need not show a court). *See also* David and Saul; Herod, feast of
> Courtroom. *See* Law court
> Dancing. [See the discussion of dancing terms in XIII.5.c. above]
> Domestic music. *See* Informal music-making
> Epiphany celebration (Twelfth Night), music at
> Execution, music at (martyrdom, etc.)
> Funeral, music at
> Garden music (music performed in a cultivated outdoor space often, but not necessarily, enclosed). *See also* Virgin and Child—In garden
> Garden of Love. *See* Musical couple
> Gladiatorial combat, music at. *See* Athletic event, music at
> Heaven. *See* Angel musician; Angel musician, wingless; Blessed; Putto musician; Putto musician, wingless

House music. *See* Informal music-making

Harvesting. *See* Rustic music

Hunting

Informal music-making (music, solo or ensemble, performed by middle- or
upper-class urban dwellers, not in a courtly setting; opposed to music in
academy, church, court, and tavern, and to military and rustic music)

Informal music-making indoors

Informal music-making outdoors. *See also* Garden music

Instruction, dance

Instruction, musical. *See also* Text, didactic—Music

Investiture, knightly

Joust. *See* Tournament or joust

Law court

Masquerade (costumed figures, no masks necessary). *See also* Theater;
Theatrical spectacle with music

Mass. *See* Ceremony, religious—Judaeo-Christian. For pictures of actual
compositions, *see* Mass and Office

Meal, music at. *See also* Symposium

Medicine and music

Middle-class music. *See* Informal music-making

Military subjects (armies marching, battle scenes, military fanfares, music
played by soldiers, etc.). *See also* Castle of Love, siege of; Ship, music in

Music school. *See* Instruction, musical

New Year's celebration, music at

Paradise. *See* Angel musician; Angel musician, wingless; Blessed; Putto musician; Putto musician, wingless; Virgin—Assumption; Virgin—Coronation;
etc.

Parnassus. *See also* Apollo and Muses; Muses

Poet as creator (the poet shown with his muse, inspiration, or genius, or being adored for his creativity)

Procession—Entrée

        Religious

Rustic music (music performed by peasants or in a rural setting). *See also*
Shepherd musician

Sacrifice, pagan. *See* Ceremony, religious—Pagan

School of music. *See* Instruction, musical

Serenade (street music not played by street musicians)

Ship, music in

Street cry

Symposium, ancient Greek, music at

Tavern music (music, solo or ensemble, performed by lower-, middle-, or
upper-class musicians in a tavern, i.e., a public room where food and/
or drink appears on the table)

Theatrical music. [See the discussion in XIII.6.f. above]

Tournament or joust, music at

Town music. *See* Civic music

Trial. *See* Law court

Wedding celebration, music at

XIV.
CLASSIFICATION SCHEME FOR PICTURES OF MUSICAL INSTRUMENTS

XIV.1.
Classifying instruments according to shape

XIV.1.a.
Difficulties of adopting standard terms

Each musical instrument shown in a picture is listed in a separate musical instruments file under the type of instrument and the century of origin of the picture. Thus, a user can find all fourteenth-century shawms, fifteenth-century harpsichords, and so on.

The prevalent confusion in the terminology used to describe musical instruments and the fact that standard classification schemes are naturally based on elements of construction rather than on pictures are the chief difficulties in naming the instruments depicted by artists. Instrument terminology is far from standard today, nor has it ever been. Some instruments are called by various names. An organistrum, for example, might as easily be referred to as a lira, a hurdy-gurdy, a vielle à roue, a chifonie or a symphonie. On the other hand, a single term sometimes designates various instruments. Thus, lira may refer to an organistrum or a sort of rebec with pegboard rather than pegbox; a lira da braccio is a type of fiddle with drone strings; and a lyra can be one of a number of varieties of lyre, although Tinctoris used the term to mean lute. Moreover, some instrument names, like lira da braccio and violin, are used to describe specific instrumental types with well-defined sets of characteristics, while others, like zither, are very broad and refer to an instrumental family comprising a large number of variants. A process of standardization often occurs in the history of a specific instrument, but artists doubtless reflect reality in depicting many variants of even the most conventional types. Thus, many pictures show instruments that differ in relatively small ways from a full-fledged lira da braccio, and, in fact, the precise difference between a fiddle with drone strings and a true lira would be difficult to establish. But a workable classification scheme must somehow account for such discrepancies. Many terms, especially those used to describe medieval instruments, are badly understood by modern scholars because not enough information survives to interpret them confidently. No two scholars agree on the basic meanings of such word complexes as crot, crowd, cruit, crwth, rota, rote, rotta, and rotte, let alone on the nuances of difference among them.

Standard instrument classification systems cannot be used for the Index of Musical Iconography, moreover, because they are made for real instruments and based on elements of construction, for example, the shape of the bore and the kind of reed employed by wind instruments, that are not always visible in pictures.

XIV.1.b.
Summary of rules

We have had to devise a method and a terminology that (1) is capable of controlling as simply and clearly as possible a vast mass of often contradictory information; (2) tells the user as accurately as possible how the instruments in pictures look; (3) reduces to a minimum the need for guesswork and subjective interpretation on the part of the cataloguer; and (4) provides ways to keep an instrument from being lost to the user if the Index names it differently than he would.

Whenever possible instruments with like attributes are grouped under a common general term, for example, trumpet, horn, zither, and then distinctions are made among the chief variants of the main type, for example, S-shaped, folded, or straight trumpets. Each of the main types and the chief variants are defined by a list of their principal characteristics (that is, the details about them assumed to be true) and their variable features and most probable shapes, in XIV.2 (strings), XIV.3 (winds), and XIV.4 (percussion and miscellaneous) below. Finally, appendix B lists the most common names used in standard bibliographical works to describe the instruments in common use in Western Europe before 1800 and gives cross-references to the terms adopted for the Index of Musical Iconography. XIV.1.c below explains how the general term describing the instrumental family is determined; XIV.1.d describes the sets of assumed details and variable features; XIV.1.e the list of common names; and XIV.1.f outlines the correct procedure for cataloguing any instrument depicted in a work of Western art before 1800.

XIV.1.c.
Determining the general term for an instrumental family

A general term for instruments with like attributes has been adopted only after working out definitions for each type. We have made extensive use of the definitions of instrumental types found in Sybil Marcuse, *Musical Instruments: A Comprehensive Dictionary* (New York: Doubleday, 1964), but they have had to be modified to conform to a system based entirely on visual characteristics. Descriptions of instruments are broad enough to include the chief variants found in Western art before 1800 and yet specific enough to differentiate one sort of instrument from another. Thus, the term "guitar" is used to describe all plucked stringed instruments with front or rear pegs, central soundhole, and so on, and the set of assumed details makes clear how the instruments in that category differ from the similar ones called citterns. The number of such general terms has been held to a minimum in order to keep a complicated system from becoming completely unmanageable, but we have been conscious of the danger of making each category so inclusive that it would no longer be of great use to a musical scholar. Only those instruments that seem to relate to their main types both historically and technologically are listed as chief variants. The general terms are for the most part common ones that can be defined clearly yet broadly, for example, trumpet and horn rather than buisine, cleron, trompe, trompette. The modifications made to describe a variant more accurately generally refer to the external shape of the instrument, for example, S-shaped, folded, or straight trumpet, or to an easily visible mechanism, for example, bellows-blown bagpipe, or to the playing position or technique of the instrument, for example, struck psaltery, or fiddle held upright. Instruments of the same general type are thus kept together in the musical instruments file, and the user can easily see both the quantity and the variety of each type.

One example of the formulation of these general terms and their modifiers should make clear the flexibility of the system. The family of stringed instruments with neither fingerboards nor keyboards, normally plucked but sometimes bowed, was among the most difficult to handle, for it includes not only the crwth-rotta types mentioned above, but also various lyrelike instruments which scholars have described in more than one way. In the Index of Musical Iconography the principal members of this family are listed as "harp," "lyre/kithara," "northern lyre," and "zither." All of those terms except "northern lyre" are common ones and clearly distinct from one another;[1] moreover, they can all be defined in broad terms that can encompass a number of variants. The zither, for example, is defined as an instrument in which the strings are stretched over a box or bowl which serves as resonator, and the principal variants are differentiated chiefly by their shapes: ala bohemica, waisted, nonwaisted, or, because some have a bowl resonator at one end which makes them resemble lutes, lute-zither. One principal variant, a long, rectangular zither with a box resonator, has a special name, Scheitholt, and so it is listed as "Zither—

---

1. We have used the term "northern lyre" rather than the more common "round lyre" (see Hortense Panum, *Stringed Instruments of the Middle Ages*, rev. Jeffrey Pulver [London: William Reeves, n.d.], pp. 90-101 and 221-232) because not all members of the family as we have defined it are round, and the instrument does seem to have originated in northern Europe. In contradistinction to other members of the family, northern lyres sometimes do have fingerboards (entered as "Lyre, northern, with fingerboard"); there are also rare examples of Scheitholts with fingerboards (enter them in the regular way as "Zither—Scheitholt" and note the presence of a fingerboard in parentheses after the instrument name).

Scheitholt," even though it, too, differs from the others chiefly in shape and might just as easily have been termed a long, rectangular zither. Moreover, zithers built in some shapes are more commonly called psalteries, and they have been designated as such, although with sufficient cross references to make the relationship plain. Psalteries could, in fact, as easily be subsumed under the more general term zither, but in the interests of simplicity, we have preferred to give them, along with the other zither types, the monochord and the trumpet marine, entries of their own. Thus, the system represents a compromise between rigid classification according to visible technological features and common usage. A careful study of the categories should in any case reveal the principles followed and enable users who wish to form collections of their own to develop such further categories as the sources require.

In some cases generic terms have been adopted without regard for what musicians in the Middle Ages and the Renaissance actually called such instruments. Our use of the term "guitar" in preference to "ghittern" may seem anachronistic, and some of our entries under "violin" come from a period before that name was standard for the instrument. Even when the picture of an instrument is labeled by an artist with what he took to be its proper name, instruments are classified in the Index of Musical Iconography according to their external shapes and whatever other properties are visible. Thus, Sybil Marcuse, in her article on "cruit" (*Musical Instruments*, p. 134) mentions a twelfth-century instrument labeled "rotta" which consists of some thirty strings stretched across a triangular box resonator. Such an instrument corresponds to our definition of a zither, and since triangular zithers are listed as "Psaltery, triangular," we have entered it as such in the musical instruments file, although we have also included a reference to the picture in the subject entry file under "Instrument, reference to—*Rotta.*"

Some scholars may quarrel with the system on the grounds that it does not distinguish well-defined variants of a main type from similar but slightly different instruments. Liras da braccio, for example, are not differentiated from other fiddles with drone strings; and violins are distinguished chiefly by pegboxes from waisted fiddles which have pegboards, even though a more discriminating set of assumed details might isolate fully developed violins from waisted fiddles with pegboxes.[2] This policy has been maintained for two reasons: simplicity and usefulness. The discriminations made among instruments of the same type must be kept to a manageable number, and they must

---

2. To be entered as a violin, an instrument must be pictured with a scroll, pegholder and the typical violin body shape with upper, middle, and lower bouts. Bowed stringed instruments with pegboxes which do not have both of those features are entered as "Fiddle with lateral pegs," a category that is listed in addition to other fiddle categories (for example, "Fiddle, waisted"). The two instrumental types ("Violin" and "Fiddle with lateral pegs") are, however, cross-referenced.

be clear enough to enable the cataloguer to make distinctions easily and quickly. Moreover, the historian of even the most well-defined instrument needs to examine all of the closely related specimens, and slightly broader categories enable him to collect this ambiguous material with a minimum of difficulty. In truth, the pictorial evidence examined thus far suggests that instruments often vary in small details from well-defined types; if such border-line cases were each made a separate category, a classification system would soon founder in a morass of unimportant detail.

Since distinctions are based on visual characteristics of the instruments, they do not always reflect organological reality. Fifes and transverse flutes, for example, are both grouped indiscriminately under "Flute, transverse," for there is no visible difference between the two instruments. The number of fingerholes in a fipple flute cannot always be seen in a picture; but that feature is the main criterion for deciding whether such an instrument is a true recorder with eight or nine fingerholes, or a simpler flageolet or shepherd's pipe, and so all such instruments are grouped under "Fipple flute--Recorder." Since the Scheitholt differs from the string drum mainly in its playing technique, which is not always clear in a picture, both instruments are classed as "Zither--Scheitholt." Some distinctions made between various types are based on features which do not explain the principal musical, that is, aural, differences between two instruments. Fiddles are distinguished from rebecs chiefly because the former have pegboards and the latter pegboxes, although it is also true that fiddles can be waisted while rebecs never are. The differences in sound between the two instruments probably have more to do with body construction and type of string than with the way the strings are fastened. But the backs of fiddles are frequently not shown, and the material from which the strings are made is always impossible to see.

XIV.1.d.
Constructing sets of assumed details and variable features
Sets of assumed details, variable features, and possible shapes for each of the principal types of instruments are given below in XIV.2 (strings), XIV.3 (winds), and XIV.4 (percussion and miscellaneous). Every instrument labeled with a particular name has all of the features described in its set of assumed details unless information on the central card specifically contradicts that supposition. All instruments called "violin," for example, are waisted and have bouts, lateral pegs set in a scroll pegbox, four strings, a tailpiece, and a fingerboard separate from the body. An instrument exhibiting all of those characteristics but having only three strings would be described on the central card as a "violin (three strings)," but it would be entered along with the other violins in the musical instruments file. Similarly, the variable features true for the particular instrument being catalogued, including its shape, are listed on the central card, but it is filed under its generic name in the musical instruments

file unless there is a special category corresponding to its variants under the main headings in XIV.2, XIV.3, or XIV.4. Thus, three-, four-, and five-stringed waisted fiddles are all entered under "Fiddle, waisted," but they are distinguished from "Fiddle, nonwaisted." These sets of assumed details, variable features, and possible shapes explain to the user of the Index which visual characteristics are associated with each instrument name, so that he will be able to find the information he seeks even if he disagrees with the terminology.

XIV.1.e.
Most common names for instruments

Appendix B lists the most common names used in standard bibliographical works and anthologies of histories of music in pictures to describe the instruments of the Middle Ages, the Renaissance, and the Baroque era with cross references to the term, often a more general one, adopted for the Index. The lira da braccio is listed as a waisted fiddle with drone strings; chitarroni, theorboes, and theorboed lutes are all listed as archlutes; and the krummer zink is listed as an S-shaped cornett. Thus, the user can find the information he seeks, if not from the sets of assumed details in XIV.2, XIV.3, and XIV.4, then from the list of common instrument names in appendix B.

XIV.1.f.
Cataloguing instruments

(1) First, find the family name given to the instrument, either by consulting the sets of assumed details or the list of common instrument names.

(2) On the central card, before the instrument name, add the size if it is uncommon and the shape if it is pertinent. The most common shapes for various instruments are included in the sets of assumed details. Thus:

> large shawm
> small lute
> large S-shaped trumpet
> small nonwaisted fiddle

(3) In parentheses after the instrument name, list all contradictions to the assumed details as well as variable features, such as the number of strings on a fiddle. The most common variable features are included in the sets of assumed details. Thus:

> small lute (6 courses, one single and five double; played with plectrum)
> struck incurved trapezoidal psaltery (12 double courses; held on lap; two hook-shaped hammers)

(4) If a detail is unclear, leave it out. If you cannot tell whether a lute is being played by the fingers or by a plectrum, or the player's right hand is
not visible, simply omit mention of that feature. The qualifier "visible"
means that only a part of the information is available in the picture. Thus,
the phrase "six strings, five visible pegs" means that the entire peg holder
cannot be seen. And the description of the small lute above implies that
the neck does not appear in the picture, for the number of pegs is omitted,
and no mention is made of the presence of frets.

(5) After the instrument has been described, enter it by family name and the
century of origin of the picture in the musical instruments file. Thus, the
small lute described above would be entered as "lute" under the century
when it was depicted. In certain cases, where the number of examples in
any one variant seems to warrant such treatment, the entry in the musical
instruments file comprises a variant of the general type, for example, "Fiddle, nonwaisted, held upright," "Trumpet, hooked—Lituus," and so on.

(6) When you cannot see enough detail to name the instrument, or you do
not know what to call it, label it with a purely descriptive term, for example, "conical wind." All such instruments are grouped in the musical
instruments file under the modifier "Unclear." This procedure prevents
the cataloguer from having to guess the name of an instrument and force
it into a category where it may not belong. Thus, it will not be lost to a
user who would have named it differently. In this category, as in others,
the principle operates that an example should be entered in the smallest
subcategory to which it belongs with certainty. For convenience of reference, the major unclear categories are as follows:

> Unclear instrument
> Unclear keyboard
> Unclear string
> Unclear string, bowed
> Unclear string, held upright (list in addition to other categories)
> Unclear string, played left-handed (list in addition to other categories)
> Unclear string, plucked
> Unclear percussion
> Unclear wind, conical
> Unclear wind, cylindrical

(7) If the visual characteristics of an instrument in a picture can apply equally
well to two instruments, so that the cataloguer cannot tell which to call it,
both possibilities are listed on the central card, for example, "either recorder
or shawm," and both instrument names are entered in the musical instruments file so that the user can decide for himself.

(8) Some ancient instruments are called both by a Greek and a Roman name.
They are listed in the Index by a composite of both names, for example,

Aulos/Tibia and Lyre/Kithara, and the second form is cross-referenced to the main entry.

(9) The following kinds of instruments are listed as "Instruments, pseudo-" in the subject entry file in addition to being described and listed in the musical instruments file: ancient and non-Western instruments in medieval, Renaissance, and baroque sources; unreal instruments invented by an artist after a classical or other source; and parodies of real instruments, such as bowed rakes and dogs played as bagpipes, which sometimes appear in the margins of miniatures.

XIV.2.
Stringed instruments

XIV.2.a.
Introduction

The following list comprises all of the terms used to describe families of stringed instruments, along with their chief variants, currently in use in the Index of Musical Iconography. Each brief description is divided into three parts: assumed details, variable features, and possible shapes. The major variants are listed beneath the generic names. A variant is presumed to have all of the characteristics of the main type with the differences explained in its modifier or in the brief description which follows it.

XIV.2.b.
Special terms used in connection with stringed instruments

The following terms, among others, are used in describing each instrument:

(1) Types of string holder

End button. The strings are fastened to buttons on the lower rib or base of the instrument.

String fastener. A flat string holder is attached directly onto the belly or the soundboard of the instrument, as on a lute or guitar.

Strings run over soundboard. The strings run over the lower end of the belly or soundboard and are apparently fastened directly to the base of the instrument.

Tailpiece. A string holder made of wood or other material is attached to the base of the instrument by strings or by a loop of gut, as on the violin or Minnesinger fiddle.

(2) Position of the pegs

Front or rear. The pegs are attached to a pegboard or disc.

Lateral. The pegs are attached to a pegbox.

(3) Arrangement of soundholes

Central. There is one soundhole in the middle of the belly or soundboard.

Multiple. There are more than two soundholes, often in the corners of the belly or soundboard.

Paired. There are two soundholes, one on either side of the belly or soundboard. Their shape is not noted.

(4) Playing position for bowed stringed instruments (if different from the usual shoulder position)

Held horizontally. The instrument is held across the chest, and is apparently bowed vertically.

Held upright. The instrument is played with the neck at the top, as with the viol.

XIV.2.c.
Note about the backs of stringed instruments

One of the standard criteria for identifying stringed instruments before 1800 has traditionally been the shape of the instrument's back, whether it is flat or vaulted. Standard reference works correctly define a lute as having a vaulted back, a guitar a flat back. Unfortunately, this significant feature of construction can seldom be seen in pictures. Since a classification scheme based on pictures must necessarily rely entirely on visible aspects, the shape of the back can seldom aid the viewer in identifying the type of stringed instrument. However, pictures often show the sides of instruments, so that the viewer can know whether or not they are furnished with ribs. If the back of an instrument is separated from its soundboard by ribs, the back must either be flat, as on the viol, or rounded or arched as on the chitarra battente. The backs of such ribbed instruments are either parallel to their soundboards, as on the guitar, or at some angle to them, as on the cittern. If an instrument does not have ribs, its back is attached directly to the soundboard and must therefore curve around so that both parts can be joined. Thus, the visible side of an instrument like the lute implies the presence of a vaulted back, even though it cannot be seen in a picture. In the sets of assumed details, instruments with vaulted backs are differentiated from those which have backs separated from their soundboards by ribs. As with other features of construction, these details are assumed to be true for every instrument catalogued unless they are specifically contradicted in the brief descriptions on the central cards. Thus, the entry "Nonwaisted fiddle" implies that its ribs can be seen; if they cannot be seen, the entry should read "Nonwaisted fiddle (ribs not visible)," and if the back is attached directly to the soundboard, "Nonwaisted fiddle (vaulted back)."

XIV.2.d.
List of stringed instruments with assumed details and variable features

BOW, MUSICAL
Assumed details: A flexible wooden stick held under tension by a string stretched between its two ends. There are so few examples in Western art before 1800 that all are entered in one category. Note variants on the central card.

CITTERN

a   b

Assumed details: Back separated from the soundboard by ribs; winged (a) or rounded (b) shape; lateral pegs; central soundhole; end buttons and bridge; differs from guitar (q.v.) chiefly in shape
Variables: Number of strings (courses) and pegs; presence of frets; played by plectrum or fingers; sickle-shaped or plain pegbox

CITTERN—BANDORA/ORPHARION (The bandora is a large cittern-like instrument of the sixteenth and seventeenth centuries. It is distinguished from the cittern by its scalloped silhouette (c) and by the fact that it has a string fastener. The orpharion is a smaller bandora tuned like a lute.)

c

CLAVICHORD
Assumed details: Keyboard; rectangular shape; may rest on a table or stand; fretted clavichords should (but may not) show the curvature of the rear portion of the keys

CLAVICYTHERIUM
Assumed details: Upright harpsichord; strings vertical (perpendicular to keyboard)

CLAVICYTHERIUM, PORTATIVE (small enough to be carried and played by one person)

CLAVIORGANUM. See Wind Instruments [XIV.3.b. below]

FIDDLE

a   b

Assumed details: Back separated from the soundboard by ribs; shown with bow; frontal or rear pegs (pegboard not pegbox); paired sound-holes; tailpiece
Variables: Number of strings and pegs; presence of frets; playing position if upright or horizontal
Possible shapes: Waisted (e.g., a-d)
Nonwaisted (e)

c   d

FIDDLE BOWED LEFT-HANDED (list in addition to other fiddle categories)
FIDDLE, KEYED (a keyboard mechanism to stop the strings is added to the neck of the instrument)
FIDDLE, NONWAISTED
FIDDLE, NONWAISTED, HELD HORIZONTALLY
FIDDLE, NONWAISTED, HELD UPRIGHT
FIDDLE, POCKET (a kit, or tiny bowed stringed instrument in the shape of a fiddle; list in addition to fiddle shape)

e

FIDDLE, WAISTED
FIDDLE, WAISTED, HELD HORIZONTALLY
FIDDLE, WAISTED, HELD UPRIGHT
FIDDLE WITH DRONE STRING (the drone string is off the fingerboard; list in addition to other fiddle categories)
FIDDLE WITH LATERAL PEGS (list in addition to other fiddle categories).
See also Violin

GUITAR
>Assumed details: Back separated from the soundboard by ribs; front or
>rear pegs; central soundhole; string fastener; differs from cittern (q.v.)
>chiefly in shape
>
>Variables: Number of strings (courses) and pegs; presence of frets; played
>by plectrum or fingers
>
>Possible shapes: Waisted or nonwaisted. For some shapes, *see* Fiddle

GUITAR, NONWAISTED

GUITAR, WAISTED

GUITAR WITH THUMB HOLE (neck folds back on itself leaving a hole for
the left thumb; list in addition to other guitar categories)

GUITAR WITH VAULTED BACK (list in addition to other guitar categories)

HARP
>Assumed details: Strings run perpendicular to the resonator
>
>Variables: Number of strings; presence of pegs; held by a band or not;
>since the shape of the soundbox is often not clearly enough depicted
>in pictures, variants are not noted; presence of pedals
>
>Possible shapes: Angular (the soundbox and neck form an angle, and
>there is no pillar: a); arched (the neck projects from the soundbox
>and arches over it to form the neck: b); frame (strings are enclosed
>by a triangular frame consisting of soundbox, neck, and pillar: c)

a

b

HARP, ANGULAR

HARP, ARCHED

HARP, FRAME

HARP, FRAME—DOUBLE (two rows of strings)

HARP, FRAME—HOOK (hooks are set into the neck; when one is pressed
against a string, the pitch is raised by a semitone)

HARP, FRAME—TRIPLE (three rows of strings)

c

HARPSICHORD
>Assumed details: Keyboard; wing shape (that is, like a grand piano, or
>an incurved demi-trapezoid); may rest on stand or table; legs not
>fastened directly to instrument
>
>Variables: Number of keyboards

HARPSICHORD, DOUBLE (two manuals, one above the other)

LUTE
>Assumed details: Vaulted back; lateral pegs; bent-back pegbox; central
>soundhole; string fastener
>
>Variables: Number of strings (courses) and pegs; presence of frets;
>played by plectrum or fingers

LUTE, ARCH- (a bass lute with open bass strings placed off-board and se-
cured to a separate pegbox, as in the chitarrone, theorbo, and theor-
bo-lute)

LUTE, LONG (a lute with a very small body in relation to the length of its
neck, as in the colascione)

LUTE PLAYED LEFT-HANDED (list in addition to other lute categories)

LUTE, STRAIGHT-NECKED (neck not bent back at pegbox)

LYRE/KITHARA
>Assumed details: A yoke consisting of two arms and connected by a
>crossbar projects from a soundbox; the strings run from the sound-
>box to the crossbar
>
>Variables: Number of strings; presence of pegs; played by plectrum or
>fingers; held by a band or not

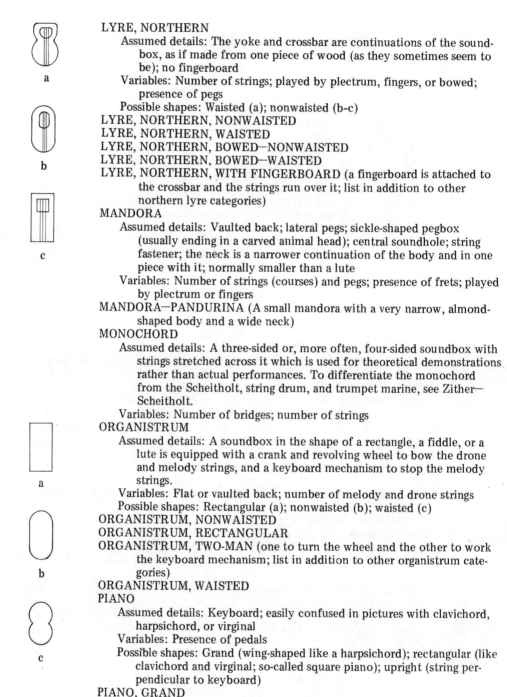

LYRE, NORTHERN
  Assumed details: The yoke and crossbar are continuations of the sound-box, as if made from one piece of wood (as they sometimes seem to be); no fingerboard
  Variables: Number of strings; played by plectrum, fingers, or bowed; presence of pegs
  Possible shapes: Waisted (a); nonwaisted (b-c)
LYRE, NORTHERN, NONWAISTED
LYRE, NORTHERN, WAISTED
LYRE, NORTHERN, BOWED—NONWAISTED
LYRE, NORTHERN, BOWED—WAISTED
LYRE, NORTHERN, WITH FINGERBOARD (a fingerboard is attached to the crossbar and the strings run over it; list in addition to other northern lyre categories)
MANDORA
  Assumed details: Vaulted back; lateral pegs; sickle-shaped pegbox (usually ending in a carved animal head); central soundhole; string fastener; the neck is a narrower continuation of the body and in one piece with it; normally smaller than a lute
  Variables: Number of strings (courses) and pegs; presence of frets; played by plectrum or fingers
MANDORA—PANDURINA (A small mandora with a very narrow, almond-shaped body and a wide neck)
MONOCHORD
  Assumed details: A three-sided or, more often, four-sided soundbox with strings stretched across it which is used for theoretical demonstrations rather than actual performances. To differentiate the monochord from the Scheitholt, string drum, and trumpet marine, see Zither—Scheitholt.
  Variables: Number of bridges; number of strings
ORGANISTRUM
  Assumed details: A soundbox in the shape of a rectangle, a fiddle, or a lute is equipped with a crank and revolving wheel to bow the drone and melody strings, and a keyboard mechanism to stop the melody strings.
  Variables: Flat or vaulted back; number of melody and drone strings
  Possible shapes: Rectangular (a); nonwaisted (b); waisted (c)
ORGANISTRUM, NONWAISTED
ORGANISTRUM, RECTANGULAR
ORGANISTRUM, TWO-MAN (one to turn the wheel and the other to work the keyboard mechanism; list in addition to other organistrum categories)
ORGANISTRUM, WAISTED
PIANO
  Assumed details: Keyboard; easily confused in pictures with clavichord, harpsichord, or virginal
  Variables: Presence of pedals
  Possible shapes: Grand (wing-shaped like a harpsichord); rectangular (like clavichord and virginal; so-called square piano); upright (string perpendicular to keyboard)
PIANO, GRAND

PIANO, RECTANGULAR
PIANO, UPRIGHT
PSALTERY

> Assumed details: A zither (q.v.) in one of a number of special shapes
>
> Variables: Number of strings (courses); held horizontally (long end to one side), upright (long end at top), or in lap; played by plectrum or fingers or struck with sticks or hooks
>
> Possible shapes: Trapezoidal (a); demi-trapezoidal (b); incurved trapezoidal (c); incurved demi-trapezoidal (d); rectangular (e); triangular (f)

PSALTERY, DEMI-TRAPEZOIDAL
PSALTERY, DOUBLE (strung on both sides; list in addition to other psaltery categories)
PSALTERY, HARP- (An instrument constructed like a frame harp [q.v.] but with a soundboard behind the strings)
PSALTERY, INCURVED DEMI-TRAPEZOIDAL
PSALTERY, INCURVED TRAPEZOIDAL
PSALTERY, RECTANGULAR
PSALTERY, SQUARE
PSALTERY, STRUCK (that is, a dulcimer; list in addition to other psaltery categories)
PSALTERY, TRAPEZOIDAL
PSALTERY, TRIANGULAR
REBEC

> Assumed details: Vaulted back; shown with bow; lateral pegs; paired soundholes; tailpiece; neck is one piece with body (or split-level soundboard); no frets
>
> Variables: Number of strings and pegs; playing position if upright or horizontal; neck if bent back

REBEC BOWED LEFT-HANDED (list in addition to other rebec categories)
REBEC, POCKET (a ket, or tiny bowed stringed instrument in the shape of a rebec)
SPINET

> Assumed details: Keyboard; polygonal, pentagonal, or leg-of-mutton shape in which strings proceed diagonally from left to right of player; set on stand or table; legs not directly attached to instrument

TRUMPET MARINE

> Assumed details: A three-sided or four-sided soundbox with one, two, or more strings stretched across it; shown with bow. To differentiate the trumpet marine from the monochord, Scheitholt, and string drum, see under Zither-Scheitholt
>
> Variables: Held upright or bottom up; number of strings

VIOL

> Assumed details: Back separated from the soundboard by ribs; waisted shape; shown with bow; lateral pegs; paired soundholes; tailpiece; fretted; all sizes played upright; the player is seated (since the lyra viol cannot be distinguished from other types in pictures, no special category has been made for it)
>
> Variables: Number of strings and pegs

VIOL—BARYTON (an instrument like a bass viol but with additional strings that pass close to the belly and under the neck so that they may be plucked with the thumb and sound sympathetically)

a

b

c

d

e

f

a

VIOLIN

 Assumed details: Back separated from the soundboard by ribs; waisted shape, with upper, middle, and lower bouts (a); shown with bow; lateral pegs and scroll pegholder; paired soundholes; tailpiece; no frets; four strings; played on shoulder. *See also* Fiddle with lateral pegs

VIOLIN, POCKET (a kit, or tiny bowed stringed instrument in the shape of a violin

VIOLIN—VIOLA (a larger violin; it is often not possible to distinguish between violas and violins in pictures)

VIOLONCELLO

 Assumed details: Same as for violin save that the player is seated, and the instrument has an end pin

VIOLONE

 Assumed details: Back separated from the soundboard by ribs; waisted shape; shown with bow; lateral pegs; paired soundholes; tailpiece; end pin; no frets; the player stands to play it. This category includes both double bass and double bass viol, both of which require the player to stand.

 Variables: Number of strings and pegs

VIRGINAL

 Assumed details: Rectangular shape with keyboard set at one corner of long side, not usually in the center; set on a stand or table; legs not fastened directly to instrument

VIRGINAL, DOUBLE (a smaller virginal is housed in a recess of the larger one; when the smaller one is not being played its keyboard is visible next to the larger one; when the smaller one is being played it often sets on top of the larger one)

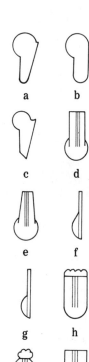

a   b

c   d

e   f

g   h

i   j

ZITHER

 Assumed details: The strings are stretched over a box or a bowl which serves as resonator. The instrument has neither neck nor fingerboard and the strings are normally plucked unstopped [but see Zither, lute-below]. The psaltery is a species of zither; psalteries are distinguished from zithers only by their shapes [q.v.].

ZITHER—ALA BOHEMICA

 Assumed details: Zither in the form of a long rectangle with a circular head: a-c; held upright

 Variables: Number of strings (courses); played by plectrum or fingers; presence of pegs

ZITHER, BOWED (list in addition to other categories)

ZITHER, LUTE-

 Assumed details: Zither in which the strings are stretched over a board at the lower end of which is a bowl-shaped resonator (front view: d-e; side view: f-g); held upright; frontal or rear pegs

 Variables: Number of strings; played by plectrum or fingers

ZITHER, NONWAISTED

 Assumed details: All nonwaisted zithers that are not in the form of an ala bohemica, lute, or Scheitholt.

 Variables: Arrangement of soundholes; number of strings (courses); played by plectrum, finger, or bow

 Possible shapes: Apparently no standardized ones (h-j, etc.)

ZITHER—SCHEITHOLT
Assumed details: Long rectangular zither with box resonator (front
view: k; side view: l); The Scheitholt was apparently strummed by
the right hand while a small stick held in the left stopped the strings.
The string drum, which is identical in shape, was played by striking
all the strings, which thus became drones, with a small stick. Since
the playing technique cannot be distinguished in pictures, they are
classified together. The Scheitholt is distinguished from the rectangular psaltery (q.v.) by the fact that it has fewer strings and a narrower
body; it is distinguished from the monochord (q.v.) by the fact that
it usually has more strings and is seen in actual performances rather
than theoretical demonstrations; it is distinguished from the trumpet
marine (q.v.) by the fact that it has a four-sided box resonator and
is not bowed.
Variables: Number of strings; type of string holder; presence of frets for
some or all strings; struck with stick or not

k

l

ZITHER, WAISTED
Assumed details: Any waisted zither-type instrument
Variables: Number of strings (courses); played by plectrum, fingers, or
bow; arrangement of soundholes
Possible shapes: Apparently no standardized ones (m-o, etc.)

m

n

XIV.3.
Wind instruments

o

XIV.3.a.
Introduction

The following list comprises all of the terms used to describe families of
wind instruments, along with the chief variants of each, currently in use in
the Index of Musical Iconography. Each brief description is divided into three
parts: assumed details, variable features, and possible shapes. The major variants are listed beneath the generic names. A variant is presumed to have all of
the characteristics of the main type with the differences explained in its modifier or in the brief description following it. The main criteria for determining
the character of many wind instruments are the shape of the tube and, when
visible, the type of mouthpiece, that is, cup, fipple, reed, and so on. Wind
instruments have in general fewer variable features than strings; often the
principal variable feature is the number of the fingerholes, which rarely can
be counted accurately.

XIV.3.b.
List of wind instruments with their assumed details and variable features

AULOS/TIBIA
Assumed details: Slender tube, more cylindrical than conical; reeds are
often visible; no bell or flare; fingerholes
Variables: Number of fingerholes
AULOS/TIBIA, DOUBLE (two pipes, either parallel or divergent)

a

AULOS/TIBIA, PHRYGIAN (double pipes in which one pipe is straight and
    the other has a turned-up end: a)
AULOS/TIBIA, PHRYGIAN, WITH ROTARY RINGS (Phrygian auloi with
    knoblike projections on their pipes, which are probably for turning
    rotary rings that allow the fingerholes to be opened or closed)
BAGPIPE
    Assumed details: Animal-skin bag held under the player's arm
    Variables: Number of chanter and drone pipes, and whether they are
        cylindrical or conical or in hornpipe shape
BAGPIPE, BELLOWS-BLOWN(bellows are used instead of player's breath
    to fill bag)
BASSOON (ca. 1650 on)
    Assumed details: Conical tube widest at top; may be shown as a separately
        jointed tube doubled back on itself, bell extending above mouthpiece
        end; crook mouthpiece; fingerholes. *See also* Curtal
    Variables: Number of fingerholes; number of keys
BLADDER PIPE
    Assumed details: Balloonlike bladder placed between blowpipe and main
        tube
    Variables: Cylindrical or conical tube; number of fingerholes
    Possible shapes: Curved or straight
BLADDER PIPE, CURVED
BLADDER PIPE, STRAIGHT
CHALUMEAU. According to Marcuse, *Musical Instruments*, p. 87, this was
    the name given to any rustic reedpipe and specifically to one with a
    single reed, like a clarinet. Since the reed cannot be seen in pictures,
    chalumeaux catalogued in the Index will most likely be analyzed as
    "Unclear wind, cylindrical," or perhaps occasionally as "Flute, fipple—
    Recorder." Marcuse states that the chalumeau was transformed in the
    eighteenth century into the clarinet.
CLARINET
    Assumed details: Tube more cylindrical than conical; small bell; single
        reed sometimes visible; fingerholes
    Variables: Number of fingerholes; number of keys
CLAVIORGANUM
    Assumed details: Combination of organ and stringed keyboard instru-
        ment
    Variables: Number of keyboards and pipes; number of stops
CORNETT
    Assumed details: Cup or funnel mouthpiece; tube more conical than
        cylindrical; no bell or flare; fingerholes
    Variables: Octagonal or round tube; number of fingerholes
    Possible shapes: Curved (a); S-shaped (b); straight (c); serpentine (d)
CORNETT, CURVED
CORNETT—SERPENT (bass cornett)
CORNETT, S-SHAPED
CORNETT, STRAIGHT
CRUMHORN
    Assumed details: Tube more cylindrical than conical; turned-up end; reed
        cap; no bell or flare; fingerholes
    Variables: Number of fingerholes

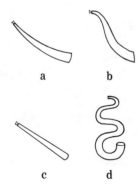

a   b

c   d

CURTAL

    Assumed details: Tube more conical than cylindrical; conical tube widest at top; unjointed tube in one piece; crook mouthpiece emerges from top of instrument; sometimes a slightly flared bell at top; fingerholes. *See also* Bassoon

    Variables: Number of fingerholes

FLUTE, FIPPLE—RECORDER

    Assumed details: Tube more cylindrical than conical; tube usually shown as cylindrical even though bore is slightly conical, widest at top; the taper toward the bottom became more pronounced after ca. 1650; may be shown as separately jointed tube after ca. 1650; fipple in one side of tube sometimes visible; beaked mouthpiece sometimes visible; usually ends in slight flare or bell; fingerholes. Except for tabor pipes, all tubes with fipples are listed as recorders, regardless of the number of fingerholes, e.g., flageolets, shepherds' pipes, etc.

    Variables: Number of fingerholes; presence of fontanelle or crook mouthpiece

FLUTE, FIPPLE—RECORDER, DOUBLE (two pipes)

FLUTE, FIPPLE—TABOR PIPE. *See* Pipe and tabor

FLUTE—PANPIPES

    Assumed details: Several cylindrical pipes joined together or carved of a single block of stone or wood; no fingerholes

    Variables: Number of pipes

    Possible shapes: Bowl (a); Raft (b); Rectangular (c)

a

FLUTE—PANPIPES, BOWL-SHAPED

FLUTE—PANPIPES, RAFT-SHAPED

FLUTE—PANPIPES, RECTANGULAR

b

FLUTE, PREHISTORIC

    Assumed details: Often made of bone; no flare or bell; normally end blown

    Variables: With or without fingerholes

c

FLUTE, TRANSVERSE

    Assumed details: Side blown; usually cylindrical tube; conical tube, wider at blowing end, appears ca. 1680; fingerholes. Fifes are included in this category.

    Variables: Number of fingerholes; number of keys

HORN

    Assumed details: Cup mouthpiece; tube more conical than cylindrical; no fingerholes; no bell or flare except on coiled horn; shorter than trumpet (very long horn types are listed as conical trumpets [q.v.])

    Possible shapes: Coiled (a); curved (b); S-shaped (c); straight (d)

a

HORN, COILED

HORN, CURVED

HORN, CURVED—OLIPHANT (a short, thick, curved horn of ivory, sometimes an elephant tusk, usually elaborately carved)

HORN, S-SHAPED

HORN, STRAIGHT

b   c

HORNPIPE

    Assumed details: Tube more cylindrical than conical; turned-up conical bell of cowhorn (or shaped like a cowhorn); the reed may be enclosed in another conical cowhorn; fingerholes

    Variables: Number of fingerholes

d

HORNPIPE, DOUBLE (two parallel pipes, often shown tied together; indicate whether two separate bells or one common bell)

OBOE (ca. 1660 on)

Assumed details: Tube more conical than cylindrical; tube narrower and with less taper than shawm; separately jointed tube; no pirouette; smaller bell with narrower flare than shawm; fingerholes

Variables: Number of fingerholes; number of keys

ORGAN, HYDRAULIC

Assumed details: In antiquity, usually shown as a set of vertical pipes mounted on a box or short, thick column; men may work pumps on either side. In the Middle Ages, barrellike water cisterns and men working the pumps are usually shown.

Variables: Number of pipes

ORGAN, LARGE

Assumed details: The position of the keyboard(s) and pipes are fixed in the church or hall

Variables: Number of keyboards and stops; presence of pedals

ORGAN, PORTATIVE

Assumed details: Small portable organ simultaneously held and played by one person

Variables: Number of pipes; buttons for keys

ORGAN, POSITIVE

Assumed details: Movable organ set on the ground or on a table and played by one person while another works the bellows

Variables: Number of stops and pipes; presence of pedals

ORGAN, REGAL

Assumed details: Positive organ with pipes having no or extremely short resonators (tubes) so that the reeds alone speak

PIPE AND TABOR

Assumed details: For the assumed details of the tabor, *see* Drum, cylindrical in the list of percussion instruments (XIV.4.b). The pipe is usually shown as cylindrical, although it may be slightly conical, being wider at the top; the tube is usually more slender than a recorder; ranges in length from very short to very long; fipple sometimes visible; beaked mouthpiece sometimes visible; usually does not end in flare or bell; normally has three fingerholes

PIPE AND TABOR—PIPE ALONE (listed only when the three fingerholes are clearly visible or when only two holes show in the front of the instrument; otherwise, list as recorder)

PIPE AND TABOR WITH SNARE

RACKET

Assumed details: For the assumed details of the tabor, *see* Drum, cylincylinder; reed, pirouette, and/or crook may be visible; fingerholes

Variables: Number of fingerholes

RACKET—TARTOLD (large rackets with metal bodies, painted like dragons, terminating in open mouths that serve as bells)

SHAWM

Assumed details: Tube more conical than cylindrical; one-piece, unjointed tube; reed or pirouette sometimes visible; flared bell; fingerholes

Variables: Number of fingerholes; presence of fontanelle

SHAWM, DOUBLE (two pipes)

SHAWM, REED-CAPPED

TROMBONE
   Assumed details: Cup mouthpiece; tube more cylindrical than conical;
      flared or funnel bell; no fingerholes; like folded slide trumpet except
      that the loop of tube extends behind the player's head
TRUMPET
   Assumed details: Cup mouthpiece; tube more cylindrical than conical;
      flared or funnel bell; no fingerholes

   Possible shapes: Curved (a); folded (b); G-shaped (c); hooked (d); looped
      (e); S-shaped (f); straight (g)

a

TRUMPET, CONICAL, CURVED (like a curved horn, but longer)
TRUMPET, CONICAL, STRAIGHT (like a straight horn, but longer)
TRUMPET, CURVED

TRUMPET, FOLDED
TRUMPET, G-SHAPED—CORNU (ancient Roman trumpet, sometimes with

b

   wooden bar set across the diameter to strengthen the instrument
   structurally and to serve as a hand hold; normally played with one
   end resting on player's left shoulder, while the other end is held by
   his left hand, bell forward)

TRUMPET, HOOKED—CARNYX (long, hooked bronze trumpet; the bell

c

   is decorated with an animal's head; the player holds the instrument
   upright with the bell well above his head)
TRUMPET, HOOKED—LITUUS (differs from a carnyx by having an un-

   decorated bell and because it is played horizontally, the bell at a
   level with the player's head or lower)

d

TRUMPET, LOOPED
TRUMPET, SLIDE (when a player's hand is close to the mouthpiece, the

   instrument may be a slide trumpet and should be listed as such in
   addition to the other trumpet categories)

TRUMPET, S-SHAPED
TRUMPET, STRAIGHT

e

XIV.4.
Percussion instruments and miscellaneous instruments

f

XIV.4.a.
Introduction

   The following list comprises all of the terms used to describe families of
percussion instruments, along with the chief variants of each, and two miscellaneous terms, Jew's harp and mechanical instrument, currently in use in

g

the Index of Musical Iconography. Each brief description is divided into
three parts: assumed details, variable features, and possible shapes. The major
variants are listed beneath the generic names. A variant is presumed to have
all of the characteristics of the main type with the differences explained in
its modifier or in the brief description following it.

XIV.4.b.

List of percussion instruments and miscellaneous instruments with assumed details and variable features

BELL

>Assumed details: No visible clapper inside the bell; no clapper implied in the playing technique (i.e., the bell is sounded neither by pulling a rope nor by swinging it in one hand); the bell is not struck on the outside by a stick or hammer; may be fixed in the tower of a building
>
>Variables: Number of bells shown

BELL, CLAPPER

>Assumed details: A clapper is visible inside the bell or implied by the playing technique, e.g., the bell is sounded by pulling a rope or by swinging it in one hand
>
>Variables: Number of bells shown

BELL, CLAPPER—CHIME (a set of clapper bells suspended from a frame; note the number of bells in the set)

BELL, CLAPPER—HAND BELL (Bell[s] are swung in the musician's hand, the presence of the clapper being implied by the playing technique)

BELL, CLAPPER—IN TOWER (one or more clapper bells hang in the tower of a church, town hall, etc.)

BELL, PELLET

>Assumed details: A small vessel, usually globular, enclosing loose pellets. *See also* Rattle, vessel
>
>Variables: Number of bells shown

BELL, STRUCK

>Assumed details: The bell is struck on the outside with a stick or hammer
>
>Variables: Number of bells shown

BELL, STRUCK—CHIME (a set of struck bells suspended on a frame; note the number of bells that compose the set)

CLAPPERS

>Assumed details: A pair of objects struck together, both parts of the pair held in one hand
>
>Possible shapes: Rectangular; round

CLAPPERS, FOOT (the clappers are attached like a sandal to the player's foot)

CLAPPERS, RECTANGULAR (the picture may represent sticks or troughs)

CLAPPERS, ROUND (the picture may represent discs or hollowed vessels)

CLAPPERS, ROUND, ON STICKS

CYMBALS

>Assumed details: A pair of objects are struck together, with one part of the pair held in each hand; the objects are usually round

CYMBALS PLAYED WITH VERTICAL MOTION

CYMBALS STRUCK WITH STICK (including gongs)

DRUM, BARREL

>Assumed details: A bulging tube whose diameter is larger in the middle than at the ends (a)
>
>Variables: Number of drumsticks

a

DRUM, CYLINDRICAL

>Assumed details: A straight tube, its diameter the same throughout (b)
>
>Variables: Deep or shallow; number of drumsticks

b

DRUM, CYLINDRICAL, WITH PIPE. *See* Pipe and tabor (in list of wind
instruments, XIV.3.b above)

DRUM, CYLINDRICAL, WITH SNARE (a line representing a snare is shown
on the drumhead)

DRUM, FRAME
Assumed details: A very shallow cylindrical drum whose body is really
a hoop (c)
Variables: One or two drumheads

c

DRUM, FRAME—TAMBOURINE (a frame drum with jingles)

DRUM, FRICTION
Assumed details: The drumhead is made to vibrate by friction, usually
by a stick rubbed up and down or rotated through a hole in the
drumhead; the Rommelpot is an example

DRUM, KETTLE
Assumed details: The body is bowl or dish shaped
Variables: Number of drums shown; number of drumsticks

DRUM, STRING. *See* Zither—Scheitholt in XIV.2.d above

JEW'S HARP
Assumed details: A frame in clothespin or horseshoe form to which one
end of a flexible lamella is attached, its other end remaining free.
The player's mouth serves as resonator.

MECHANICAL INSTRUMENT (an instrument that runs by itself, i.e., is
actuated by wind, water, a clockwork, cranks, or whatever. Each
instrument in this category will have its own set of assumed details
and variable features.)

MECHANICAL INSTRUMENT—MUSICAL CLOCK (This instrument looks
like an ordinary timepiece and can therefore not be included in the
Index unless it is labeled as a clock which incorporates some auto-
matic music-making device.)

POT, BEATEN
Assumed details: A pot, sometimes with a membrane stretched across
the top, beaten with a spoon or a stick

RATTLE, COG
Assumed details: Scraped wheel whose axle serves as handle; when
whirled, a tongue fixed to the frame scrapes the teeth of the wheel

RATTLE, FRAME
Assumed details: Rattling objects are attached to a carrier against which
they strike

RATTLE, PENDANT
Assumed details: Series of rattling objects are hung from a frame

RATTLE, SLIDING
Assumed details: Objects slide back and forth in the slots of a frame

RATTLE, STICK
Assumed details: Rattling objects are strung on a bar or ring, as in the
sistrum

RATTLE, SUSPENSION
Assumed details: Perforated objects are mounted together to strike each
other when shaken, as in jingles

RATTLE, VESSEL
Assumed details: Rattling objects are enclosed in a vessel, often held by
a handle; the instrument is usually larger than a pellet bell (q.v.)

TRIANGLE
  Assumed details: A metal rod bent into the shape of a triangle and
    struck with a beater
TRIANGLE WITH JINGLES (jingles hang from the bottom of the instru-
    ment)
XYLOPHONE
  Assumed details: A series of graduated, tuned, wooden slabs laid parallel
    to each other; they are struck with a beater

APPENDICES

Aids to Cataloguing Works of Art with Musical Subjects

APPENDIX A. SAMPLE ENTRIES

1. Principles of selection

To demonstrate the principles of the Index of Musical Iconography in operation, selected works of art with musical subject matter are catalogued below. A reproduction of each object accompanies its description on a worksheet from the Index. The objects have been selected to illustrate a wide variety of cataloguing problems. The works of art comprise many different media and types of objects, prints, illustrations from books and manuscripts, paintings, sculptures, and various minor arts, and they represent a cross section of the time span covered by the Index, from the golden crown made in the 4th century B.C. (Jewelry Greek 4th c. B.C.—1) to the painting of a seventeenth-century Dutch interior (Hooch—3). For the most part the examples do not appear in the standard anthologies. In a few cases, however, relatively well-known examples have been included to demonstrate a particular facet of the Index. Thus, the treatment of the page from the "Utrecht Psalter" (MS Utrecht Univ 32—12) reveals the necessity of describing a scene carefully before it can be used as musicological evidence. And the Valois Tapestry (Heere—1) has been included to demonstrate the means for handling groups of objects, for the tapestry is based on a drawing (Caron—1), and a part of the same scene also appears in an engraving in a book (DoratMS [1573]—1). Moreover, we have tried to choose objects of some intrinsic musical interest, resisting the temptation to concentrate exclusively on angel musicians.

The central entry appears here exactly as in the Index, save that some instructions to cross-reference subject entries, normally indicated by the abbreviation "CR" in the margin, are here written out in square brackets. But no attempt has been made, for example, to expand the bibliographical references to include all of the sources where an object has already been published or discussed. As previously explained, the most efficient way to build the Index has seemed to involve processing books and articles one at a time rather than exhausting the sources of information about each work of art in turn. Thus, bibliographical references will be added gradually to the worksheets as more books are completely catalogued. Section 3 below lists all of the books used to prepare appendix A.

No further explanation of specific decisions regarding the method of cataloguing these examples seems necessary. A close study of the following worksheets in conjunction with the explanations found in the main body of this handbook should suffice to understand all aspects of the cataloguing process.

2. Selected objects catalogued in the Index of Musical Iconography

WORKSHEET

Symbol: Basses dances (n.d.)—1   Repro.: F; P

Artist: Anon.

Date/School: Ca. 1530-1538, French

Title: *S'ensuyvent plusieurs basses dances tant Communes que Incommunes* (n.p., n.d.):
    Title page

Medium: Print: Woodcut   Size:

Location: Paris, BN, Collection Rothschild, VI-3 *bis*-66

Description:
    Beneath the title is a woodcut showing four men standing and playing *recorders* of various sizes from a music book (notation not legible).
    According to LesureD, p. 176 (q.v. for a discussion of the contents of the volume), it was printed between 1530 and 1538 by Jacques Moderne in Lyons.

Bibl.: ParisBNCatRothschild I (1884) 100 (no ill.)

Subjects:
    Academy, music at (?)
    Informal music-making (indoors?)
    Moderne, Jacques (publisher/printer?)
    Music book
    Quartet
    S'ensuyvent plusieurs basses dances
    Text, didactic—Dance
    Title page

Basses dances (n.d.)—1
Courtesy of Service des Dons,
Bibliothèque nationale Paris

WORKSHEET

Symbol: BehamB—3   Repro.: B; X

Artist: Barthel Beham (1502-1540) (or his brother Hans Sebald Beham [1500-1550])
   [cross-reference the one to the other]

Date/School: 1531, German

Title: The Planets: Venus

Medium: Print: Woodcut   Size: 11 7/8 X 8 1/4 in.

Location: Boston Museum of Fine Arts, 53.127, p. 908; Paris, Louvre; London BM

Description:

   At the top of the print, Venus and Cupid ride in a chariot through the sky. On earth, in the background three musicians play (1) *cylindrical drum* (2 sticks); (2) *transverse flute* (= fife?); and (3) *trombone* in a balcony. They may be playing for three couples who can be seen in the background and who may be dancing.

   In the foreground left, a couple sings from a music book held in their laps, accompanied by a standing man playing (4) a *straight cornett*, and a seated man playing (5) a *frame harp* (ca. 11 strings). In the middle, a couple embrace. On the right, a couple play (6) *lute* (ca. 6 strings; frets; played with fingers), and (7) *viol*. The case for the lute lies on the ground, right foreground.

Bibl.:*HoytWP, fig. 3

Subjects:
   Dancing, couple (?)
   Duet [couple in right foreground]
   Eros/Cupid
   Gallery, musicians'
   Informal music making outdoors
   Instrument case: Lute
   Music as a worldly pleasure
   Music book
   Musical couple
   Planets, music associated with—Venus
   Planets, The [series]
   Quartet [group in left foreground]
   Sextet or larger ensemble [all performers in foreground]
   Singing, secular—With instruments
   Trio [group in balcony]

BehamB--3
Courtesy of Museum of Fine Arts, Boston

WORKSHEET

Symbol: Caron—1   Repro.: X

Artist: Antoine Caron (Ca. 1520-1599)

Date/School: Ca. 1573, French (school of Fontainebleau)

Title: Festival for the Polish Ambassadors

Medium: Drawing   Size:

Location: Saunderstown, R. I., Collection of Mr. and Mrs. Winslow Ames

Description:

A view of the ballet presented to the Polish ambassadors, who had come to Paris in 1573 to offer the crown of Poland to Henri III. The ballet was given in the Tuileries by Catherine de'Medici, the Queen Mother, who is shown seated among the spectators. The ballet by Baltasar de Beaujoyeulx is called "Le Ballet des Polonais."

Three couples dance. Music is apparently provided by musicians seated on a tall rock at the left, surmounted by Apollo playing (1) a *lyre/kithara*. Below him, 5 ladies are visible, playing (2) *viol* (= *unclear string*); (3) *violin*; (4) *violin*; (5) *lute*; and (6) *viol*. No details are visible for any of the instruments. From Jean Dorat's description of the ballet (see DoratMS [1573] —1) the rock apparently held 16 nymphs representing the provinces of France. The Tuileries are visible in the background. The scene depicts the social dancing following the formal ballet.

Lucas de Heere based his design for one of the Valois Tapestries on this drawing (see Heere—1).

Bibl.: *YatesVT, pl. Xb

Subjects:
    Apollo
    Ballet des Polonais, Le (Beaujoyeulx)
    Beaujoyeulx, Baltasar de
    Car or float, musician on
    Court, music at
    Dancing, couple
    Henri III, King of France [cross-reference to "France, Henri III, King of"]
    Instrument, pseudo-
    Medici, Catherine de', Queen of France [cross-reference to "France, Catherine de'Medici, Queen of"]
    Nymph musician
    Paris—Tuileries
    Quintet [5 ladies minus Apollo]
    Sextet or larger ensemble
    Theater—Stage setting—Ballet—Ballet des Polonais, Le (Beaujoyeulx)

Caron—1
Courtesy of John R. Freeman and Company

WORKSHEET

Symbol: DoratMS (1573)—1   Repro.: X

Artist: Anon.

Date/School: 1573, French

Title: Jean Dorat, *Magnificentissimi spectaculi a Regina Regum Matre in hortis suburbanis editi* (Paris, Fed. Morellus, 1573): Festival for the Polish Ambassadors

Medium: Print: Engraving   Size:

Location: Paris BN

Description:

 Dorat describes the ballet provided by Catherine de'Medici in the Tuileries in 1573 for the Polish ambassadors who had come to Paris to offer the Polish crown to Henri III ("Le Ballet des Polonais" by Baltasar de Beaujoyeulx).

 This engraving depicts the moving rock on which sat 16 nymphs representing the provinces of France. Only one of the 8 ladies shown plays a musical instrument, a *lute* (no details visible). See also Caron—1 and Heere—1.

Bibl.: *YatesVT, pl. 24c

Subjects:
 Ballet des Polonais, Le (Beaujoyeulx)
 Beaujoyeulx, Baltasar de
 Car or float, musician on
 Court, music at
 Dancing, couple
 Dorat, Jean
 Henri III, King of France [cross-reference to "France, Henri III, King of"]
 Medici, Catherine de', Queen of France [cross-reference to "France, Catherine de'Medici, Queen of"]
 Morellus, Fed. (publisher/printer)
 Nymph musician
 Paris—Tuileries
 Solo musician
 Text—Description of festival
 Theater—Stage setting—Ballet—Ballet des Polonais, Le (Beaujoyeulx)

DoratMS (1573)--1
Courtesy of Service des Dons,
Bibliothèque nationale Paris

WORKSHEET

Symbol: Enamel Italian 14th c.—1   Repro.: B; P

Artist: Anon.

Date/School: End of the 14th c.; Italian: Siena

Title: Belt: Scenes of Courtly Life (?)

Medium: Enamel   Size: 7′ 9 7/8″ long; 1 1/8″ wide

Location: Cleveland Museum of Art, John Huntington Collection, No. 51.30

Description:

   The belt of woven silver is ornamented by quatrefoils of translucent enamel on silver (in groups of three) separated by larger and more important translucent enamel plaques, 21 in number. The buckle is formed by a figurine of a woman playing (1) a *tambourine*.

   The larger enameled plaques include a great variety of picturesque figures: men and women playing (2) *incurved trapezoidal psaltery*; (3) *lutes* (at least 2 figures); (4) *demi-trapezoidal psaltery*; (5) *curved horn* (by a grotesque musician, half human and half beast), and perhaps other instruments. Some of the figures may be dancing. Some have no particular or an undiscovered significance. The smaller quatrefoils have formal leaf designs, busts of young girls, and a variety of fantastic motives. The final pendant suspended from the belt proper is decorated with a woman repulsing her lover, and another accepting hers.

Bibl.: *ClevelandMABull (March 1930) Part I, pp. 35-41; *ClevelandMACatGA, no. 91, p. 180

Subjects:
   Court, music at (?)
   Dancing, solo
   Grotesque musician
   Sextet or larger ensemble
   Solo musician

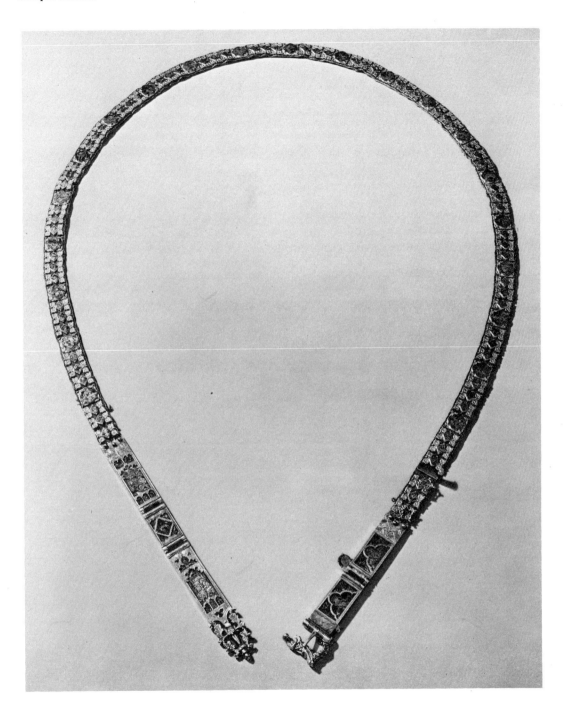

Enamel Italian 14th c.—1
Courtesy of The Cleveland Museum of Art,
Gift of the John Huntington Art
and Polytechnic Trust

See next two pages for details.

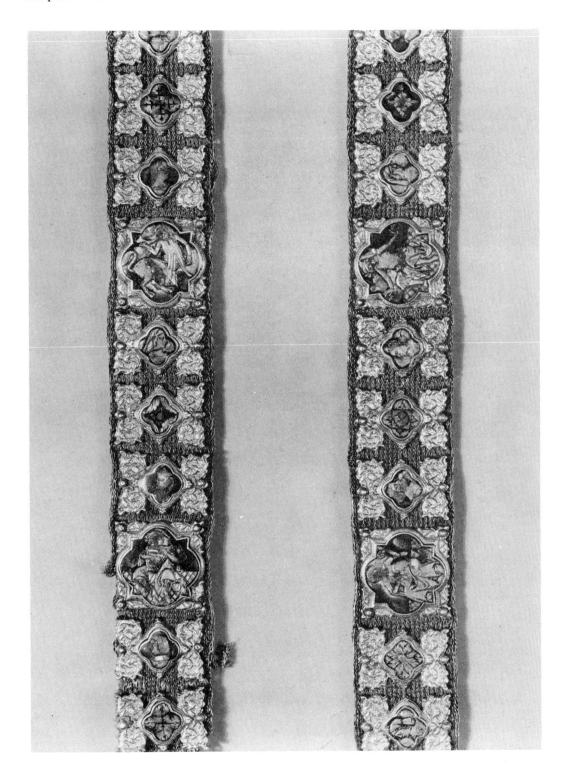

WORKSHEET

Symbol: Glass, stained Alsatian 14th c.—1   Repro.: B; X

Artist: Anon.

Date/School: Ca. 1370-1400, Alsatian

Title: Scenes from the Life of St. John the Baptist

Medium: Stained glass   Size: detail with Salome: 29 7/8 X
      16 1/8 inches

Location: Alsace, Niederhaslach, Florentiuskirche

Description:

The window shows scenes from the life of St. John the Baptist. The two upper left panels depict Herod's feast. The top center panel shows a musician playing a *nonwaisted fiddle bowed left-handed* (5 or 6 pegs). Behind him Salome carries the head of St. John the Baptist on a platter.

Bibl.: *HutterM, pl. 18 (detail); *KarlingerK, p. 489 (complete window)

Subjects:
    Court, music at
    Dancing, solo
    Herod, feast of
    Jongleur
    Meal, music at
    St. John the Baptist
    Solo musician

Glass, stained Alsatian 14th c.—1
Courtesty of Verlag Ullstein

WORKSHEET

Symbol: Guercino—1   Repro.: P; B

Artist: Giovanni Francesco Barbieri, called Guercino (1591-1666) [cross-reference to "Barbieri"]

Date/School: 17th c., Italian: Bologna

Title: Landscape with musicians

Medium: Painting: Panel (on copper)   Size: 35 × 47 cm.

Location: Florence, Uffizi, No. 1379

Description:

A group of 8 men and women sit on the bank of a river. Several of them play instruments: (1) *recorder*; (2) *recorder*; (3) *violin*; and (4) a long-necked *lute*. The woman in the foreground with her back to the viewer is probably playing (5) a *viol* (= *unclear bowed string*; 3 pegs visible). At least one woman may be singing.

A chariot drawn by two horses is crossing the river. The figures in the chariot may be mythological.

Bibl.: *Photo Alinari 382; *UnescoCat, p. 175, no. 447

Subjects:
    Informal music making outdoors
    Mythological figure, anon. (?)
    Quintet [without singer]
    Sextet or larger ensemble [with singer]
    Singing, secular—With instruments (?)
    Singing, solo (?)

Guercino—1
Alinari photo

WORKSHEET

Symbol: Heere—1   Repro.: X

Artist: Lucas de Heere (1534-1584)

Date/School: Ca. 1582, Flemish

Title: Valois Tapestries: Entertainment for the Polish Ambassadors (1573)

Medium: Tapestry   Size: 3.81 X 4.02 meters

Location: Florence, Uffizi

Description:

According to YatesVT, p. 103, Heere may have designed the tapestries for William of Orange to give to Catherine de'Medici, the Queen Mother of France, and Henri III as an appeal on behalf of François, duc d'Anjou, when he became Count of Flanders and Duke of Brabant. The scene shows one of the entertainments prepared for the Polish ambassadors who came to Paris in 1573 to offer the crown of their country to Henri III. Catherine offered a ballet at the Tuileries, which included 16 nymphs, representing the provinces of France, sitting on a moving rock from which they descended to dance the "Ballet des Polonais" designed by Baltasar de Beaujoyeulx. The tapestry depicts the social dancing after the formal ballet.

Heere's design for the tapestry is based on a drawing by Antoine Caron (see Caron—1) of the actual event. As in the Caron drawing, the rock is shown with Apollo at the top, playing (1) a *lyre/kithara*. Beneath him are 5 of the 16 nymphs, playing (2) *curved cornett*; (3) *violoncello* (4 strings; overhand bowing); (4) *violoncello* (4 strings; overhand bowing); (5) *lute* or *cittern* (3 strings; frets); and (6) *violoncello*. In Caron's drawing the rock is on the left; in Heere's tapestry it is on the right.

The Queen Mother is seated in the middle of the tapestry, and the Tuileries may be seen in the background. Three couples are shown dancing in the middle foreground. One of the men may be Henri III. A figure in the foreground may be Anne, duc de Joyeuse, possibly conversing with the head of the Polish group, Prince Albertus Laski.

See also Caron—1 and DoratMS (1573)—1

Bibl.: *YatesVT, pl. IV and pl. 24a (detail of rock); WinternitzMI, pl. 95c (detail of rock)

Subjects:

Anne, duc de Joyeuse [cross-reference
  to "Joyeuse, Anne, duc de"]
Apollo
Ballet des Polonais, Le (Beaujoyeulx)
Beaujoyeulx, Baltasar de
Car or float, musician on
Court, music at
Dancing, couple
François, duc d'Anjou, Count of Flanders,
  Duke of Brabant [cross-reference to
  "Anjou," "Flanders," and "Brabant"]
Henri III, King of France [cross-reference
  to "France, Henri III, King of"]
Instrument, pseudo-

Laski, Prince Albertus
Medici, Catherine de', Queen of France
  [cross-reference to "France, Catherine
  de'Medici, Queen of"]
Nymph musician
Paris—Tuileries
Quintet [5 ladies minus Apollo]
Sextet or larger ensemble
Tapestries, Valois [cross-reference to
  "Valois Tapestry"]
Theater—Stage setting—Ballet—Ballet
  des Polonais, Le (Beaujoyeulx)
William of Orange [cross-reference
  to "Orange, William of"]

Heere—1

WORKSHEET

Symbol: Hooch—3   Repro.: B; P

Artist: Pieter de Hooch (1629-ca. 1683)

Date/School: Ca. 1665-1668, Dutch

Title: The Music Party

Medium: Painting: Panel   Size: 39 1/2 × 46 7/8 in.

Location: Cleveland Museum of Art, No. 51.355

Description:

In a well-appointed room, a family makes music together around a table. The son plays (1) a *recorder*; the daughter (2) a rounded *cittern* (frets); and the father (3) a *violin*. The mother sits holding an open music book in her lap, beating time with her right hand. She may be singing. Several more music books lie on the table, and (4) a *viol* (frets; 3 pegs visible) rests against a chair.

A nurse and two younger children are visible through an open door in the background.

Bibl.: *ClevelandMABull (June 1952), inside front cover; *ClevelandMACatH (1966), p. 126

Subjects:

    Conducting

    Informal music-making indoors

    Music book

    Quartet [with singer]

    Singing, secular—With instruments (?)

    Singing, solo (?)

    Trio [without singer]

Hooch—3
Courtesy of The Cleveland Museum of Art,
Gift of Hanna Fund

See next page for detail.

WORKSHEET

Symbol: Jewelry Greek 4th c. B.C.—1   Repro.: B

Artist: Anon.

Date/School: 4th c. B.C., Greek in Balkans

Title: Ariadne and Dionysus

Medium:Sculpture: Jewelry (Gold diadem)   Size:

Location: New York, Metropolitan Museum of Art, Rogers Fund, 1906, No. 06.1217
    (said to have been found at Madytos in the Hellespont)

Description:

    In the middle of the crown sit Dionysus and Ariadne. On either side of them are pairs of figures: one person playing (1) a *frame harp* on the left and another on the right; one nonmusical person on the left and another on the right; and one person playing (2) *lyre/kithara* on the left and another on the right.

Bibl.: *NewYorkMetCatGM, no. 13

Subjects:
    Ariadne
    Bacchus/Dionysus
    Quartet

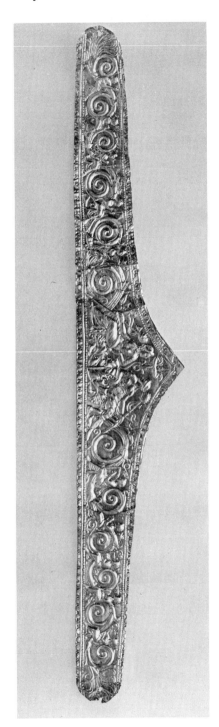

Jewelry Greek 4th c. B.C.—1
Courtesy of The Metropolitan Museum of Art,
Rogers Fund, 1906

WORKSHEET

Symbol: MS Cassel LB poet. et rom. fol. 1–2   Repro.: X

Artist: Anon.

Date/School: 1334, German

Title: Wolfram von Eschenbach, Ulrich von Türlin, Ulrich von Türheim, *Willehalm*:
    Welcoming Banquet on the Island of Montanar

Medium: MS illumination   Size: 41.5 × 29 cm.

Location: Olim Cassel, Murhard'sche und Landesbibl., Willehalm Codex, fol. 37^V (destroyed in World War II)

Description:

The MS was copied for Landgraf Heinrich von Hessen in 1334. The illuminations from fol. 30 on were never finished.

The Count and Countess of Montanar offer Willehalm and his party a banquet. Seated at the table are: Arabel (wife of Willehalm's enemy, Tybalt), the Count and Countess of Montanar, Willehalm, and two young ladies.

In front of the table stand two servants with food and three musicians playing (1) *angular harp* (= *harp-psaltery*?; the strings were never drawn); (2) *nonwaisted fiddle held horizontally* (only the back is visible, not the ribs, pegs, or strings); and (3) *shawm* (= *unclear conical wind*).

Bibl.: *FreyhanIC, pl. 37

Subjects:
    Arabel (in Willehalm)
    Court, music at
    Heinrich, Landgraf von Hessen [cross-reference to "Hessen, Heinrich, Landgraf von"]
    Jongleur
    Meal, music at
    Montanar, Count and Countess of (in Willehalm)
    Montanar, Island of (in Willehalm)
    Text, literary—Romance or epic
    Trio
    Ulrich von Türheim—Willehalm [cross-reference to "Türheim, Ulrich von"]
    Ulrich von Türlin—Willehalm [cross-reference to "Türlin, Ulrich von"]
    Wolfram von Eschenbach—Willehalm [cross-reference to "Eschenbach, Wolfram von"]

MS Cassel LB poet. et rom. fol. 1—2
Courtesy of Bildarchiv Foto Marburg

WORKSHEET

Symbol: MS New York PL Spencer 26—4   Repro.: X

Artist: Anon.

Date/School: First half of the 14th c., English

Title: Tickhill Psalter: Triumph of David (1 Samuel 18: 6-7)

Medium: MS illumination   Size:

Location: New York Public Library, Spencer Collection, MS 26, fol. 17

Description:

David, holding the head of Goliath, returns from killing the giant and is acclaimed by the women of Israel. At the left, the women play (1) two *straight trumpets*; (2) an *unclear bowed string* (3 strings; end button); and (3) a *rebec* or *nonwaisted fiddle* (ribs not visible; 3 strings; 3 visible pegs). At the right, women play (4) a *waisted guitar with thumbhole* (plectrum; 3 strings; paired soundholes; strings run over soundboard); (5) an *unclear bowed string*; and (6) two *straight trumpets*. The text reads: "egressae sunt mulieres de universis urbibus Israel, cantantes, chorosque ducentes in occursum Saul regis in tympanis laetitiae et in sistris."

Each group of women has a scroll whose wording is taken from 1 Samuel 18:7. The one on the left reads: "Percussit Saul mille [et] David dece[m] milia." The one on the right reads: "Percussit Saul mille [et] David .X. milia." (See EgbertTP, p. 25.)

Bibl.: *EgbertTP IX, figs. 61-62

Subjects:

David, triumph of

Instrument, reference to—*Sistris*
                                    Tympanis

Procession

Psalter, Tickhill [cross-reference to "Tickhill Psalter"]

Sextet or larger ensemble

Text—Bible—1 Samuel

Text—Psalter

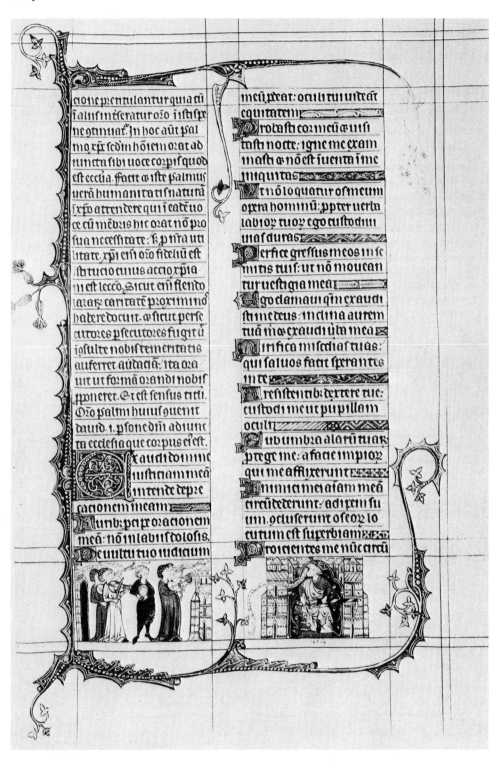

MS New York PL Spencer 26—4
Courtesy of the Spencer Collection,
The New York Public Library,
Astor, Lenox and Tilden Foundations

WORKSHEET

Symbol:MS Paris BN nouv. acq. lat. 1673—4   Repro.: X

Artist: Anon.

Date/School: 2nd half of 14th c., Italian: Lombardy

Title: Tacuinum sanitatis: The effects of instrumental music

Medium: MS illumination   Size: 32.2 × 25 cm.

Location: Paris BN MS nouv. acq. lat. 1673, fol. 86

Description:

The MS probably belonged to Verde, daughter of Bernabò Visconti (of Lombardy), and wife of Leopoldo d'Austria. The "Tacuinum" is a collection of medical information, e.g., on the influence of climate on health, the therapeutic quality of various herbs, etc.

This scene shows three musicians (= minstrels?) standing under a tree (in a garden?) playing (1) *portative organ* (ca. 13 pipes in each of 3 and sometimes 4 rows; held by a strap); (2) slightly *waisted fiddle with lateral pegs* (3 pegs visible); and (3) *shawm* (= *unclear conical wind*).

The text reads: "Organantum vel pulsare. Nature quedam in vita vel cantus violentus. melius ex eo quod est proportionatum concorditer cum voce. JUVAMENTUM: quando cantat suaviter non festinanter. NOCUMENTUM: quando discorditer cantantur quidam ipsorum alterum vix audietur oculte cantare. REMOTIO NOCUMENTI: cum proportionaliter concordatur."

Bibl.: *MalletJP, fig. 37; *ToescaTS, f. 86

Subjects:
    Garden music
    Instrument support—strap
    Medicine and music
    Minstrel (?)
    Musical term—*Organantum*
             Pulsare
    Tacuinum sanitatis
    Text, didactic—Medicine
    Trio
    Visconti, Verde

Organicum ul' pulfarc.

atur queda invita ul' cant' molent' melius erco. q' eft p̄
p̄rnonati concordicr̄ ai uoce. Jnuamentū qn cantat suaui̅
non festinantē. nocument̄ qn discordicr̄ cantat qd ipͦ.
alter̄ii uir audietur occulte cantat. r̄ene̅ no̅i. ai ͡p̄tona
liter̄ ͡cordatur.

MS Paris BN nouv. acq. lat. 1673—4
Courtesy of Service des Dons,
Bibliothèque nationale Paris

WORKSHEET

Symbol: MS Utrecht Univ 32—12   Repro.: X

Artist: Anon.

Date/School: French, 816-843 (EngelbregtUP, p. 139, dates it 850 or after)

Title: Utrecht Psalter: Psalm 80 (King James 81)

Medium: MS illumination   Size:

Location: Utrecht, Universiteitsbibliotheek, MS 32, fol. 48

Description:

    The Psalter was prepared for St. Peter's Abbey at Hautvillers (Rheims).

    DeWaldUP: "In the center of the heavens the beardless, cross-nimbed Christ-Logos is seated within a globe-mandorla. He holds an open scroll, the 'statute' and 'testimony' (Verses 5-6 [4-5]), in his left hand and is attended by six angels with wands. In the register below, the psalmist at the left exhorts a dancer and four musicians [the two at the left play (1) *curved horns* or *conical trumpets*; the two at the right play (2) *angular harp* (ca. 7 strings) and (3) *cittern*] to make 'a joyful noise' before the Lord (Verses 2-3 [1-2]: 'Sumite psalmum et date tymphanum, psalterium iocundum cum cythara / Bucinate in neomoenia tuba . . . .') in front of a tabernacle with drawn curtains revealing a hanging lamp. In the lowest register a group of horsemen, the enemy (Verse 15 [14]), is charging against the Israelites. Some of these Israelites are cutting grain, others are gathering honey from hives out of which bees are flying. These episodes are suggested by Verse 17 [16]: 'He should have fed them also with the finest of the wheat; and with honey out of the rock . . . .' The latter part of this phrase is also illustrated by Moses smiting the rock to give water to a group of men, women, and children who are beseeching him for help. At the extreme right another group is worshiping the Golden Calf (Verse 10[9])."

    See also MS Cambridge Trinity R.17.1—12.

Bibl.: DeWaldUP, pl. lxxv; *PalUP, fol. 48

Subjects:
    Christ
    Dancing, solo
    David as psalmist
    Instrument, reference to—*Cythara*
                         Psalterium
                         Tuba
                         Tymphanum
    Psalter, Utrecht [cross-reference to "Utrecht Psalter"]
    Quartet
    Text—Bible—Psalm 80 (King James 81)
    Text—Psalter

LXXX INFINEM·

EXSULTATEDOAD
IUTORINOSTRO · IUBILATE
DOIACOB·
SUMITEPSALMUMETDATE
TYMPHANUM · PSALTERIUM
IOCUNDUMCUCYTHARA ·
BUCINATEINNEOMENIATU
BA · ININSIGNIDIESOLLEM
NITATISNOSTRAE
QUIAPRAECEPTUMISRAHEL
EST ETIUDICIUDOIACOB ·
TESTIMONIUMINIOSEPHPO
SUITILLUD CUMEXIRETDE
TERRAAEGYPTI LINGUAM
QUAMNONNOUERAT
AUDIUIT;
DIUERTITABONERIBUS

PROTORCULARIB·

DORSUMEIUS · MANUSEI
INCOPHINOSERUIERUNT
INTRIBULATIONEINUOCAS
TIMEETLIBERAUITE EXAU
DIUITEINABSCONDLIOTEM
PESTATIS PROBAUITEAPUD
AQUAMCONTRADICTIO
NIS DIAPSALMA
AUDIPOPULUSMEUSETCON
TESTABORTE ISRAHELSIAU
DIERISMENONERITINTE
DSRECENSNECADORABIS
DMALIENUM;
EGOENIMSUMDNSDSTUUS
QUIEDUXITEDETERRAAE
CYPTI · DILATAOSTUUM
ETIMPLEBOILLUD ·

ASAph

ETNONAUDIUITPOPULUS·
MEUSUOCEMMEAM · ETISRA
HELNONINTENDITMIHI;
ETDIMISIEOSSECUNDUMDE
SIDERIACORDISEORUM·
IBUNTINADINUENTIONI
BUSSUIS
SIPOPULUSMEUSAUDISSET
ME · ISRAHELSIINUIISMEIS
AMBULASSET
PRONIHILOFORSITANINI
MICOSEORUMHUMILIAS·
SEM ETSUPERTRIBULAN
TESEOSMISISSEM MANUMEA
INIMICIDNIMENTITISUNT
EI · ETERITTEMPUSEORUM
INSAECULA ·

MS Utrecht Univ 32—12
Courtesy of University Library Utrecht:
Ms. 32, fol. 48 recto

WORKSHEET

Symbol: MS Vienna NB 2571—1   **Repro.: X**

Artist: Anon.

Date/School: Mid or 3rd qt. of 14th c., Italian (probably near Bologna)

Title: Bénoît de Sainte-More, Roman de Troie: King Pelias commissions Jason to bring the Golden Fleece from Colchis

Medium: MS illumination   Size: P.: 235 × 325 mm.
                                                  Min.: 195 × 64 mm.

Location: Vienna, Nationalbibliothek, MS Nr. 84, Cod. 2571, fol. 5ᵛ

Description:

   At the left, King Pelias sits on his throne flanked by four seated men. In the center stands Jason. At the right are four standing musicians, playing (1) *waisted fiddle* (neck and pegholder not visible); (2) *lute*; and (3) two *straight trumpets.*

Bibl.: *ViennaNBCatIH V², pl. liii

Subjects:

   Bénoît de Sainte-More—Roman de Troie [cross-reference to "Sainte-More, Bénoît de" and "Roman de Troie"]
   Court, music at
   Jason
   Jongleur
   Pelias, King
   Quartet
   Text, literary—Romance or epic

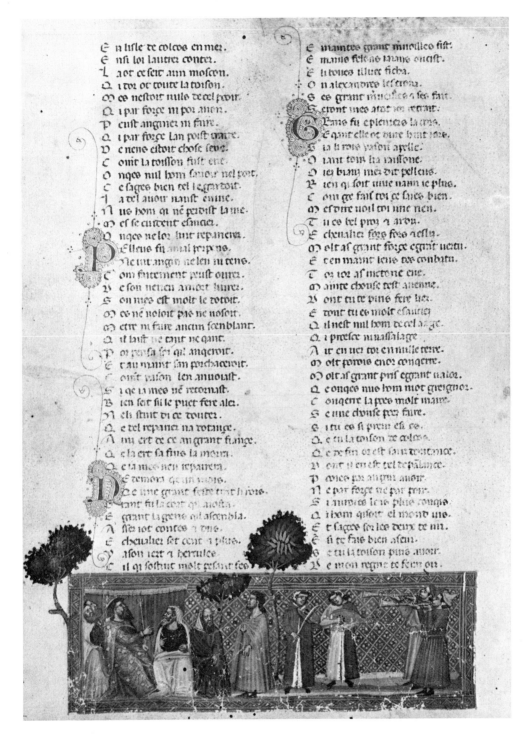

MS Vienna NB 2571—1
Courtesy of Österreichische Nationalbibliothek

See next page for detail.

WORKSHEET

Symbol: MS Zurich Zentralbibl Rheinau 15—1   Repro.: P

Artist: Anon. (The scribe was Magister Johannes)

Date/School: Ca. 1360, southwest German (ZurichSM, p. 288, says 1335-1340)

Title: Rudolph von Ems, *Weltchronik*: David and musicians (2 Samuel 6:5)

Medium: MS illumination   Size: P.: 33.5 × 22.9 cm.

Min.: 19 × 16 cm.

Location: Zurich, Zentralbibliothek, MS Rheinau 15, fol. 218^V

Description:

In a two-register architectural frame, King David sits at left playing (1) a *frame harp* (12 strings). To the right above him, a standing musician plays (2) a slightly *waisted fiddle held horizontally* (4 strings; 3 or 4 pegs); and a scribe writes the psalms. To the right below, four musicians play (3) *nonwaisted fiddle* (4 strings and pegs); (4) slightly *waisted organistrum* (2 strings; 5 keys); (5) *incurved demi-trapezoidal psaltery* (10 strings; plectrum); and (6) *harp-psaltery* (7 strings).

The text (verses 30831-30850) reads: "Leite der gottes dienstman / Allen sinen flis daran / Wie er gottes lob gemerte / Getihte und gelerte . . . / Dz er den salter tihte / Und wislich daran berihte . . . / Ze gottes lob kurtzewile vil / Mit allerhande seitenspil."

Bibl.: ZurichSM, p. 288; *Foto Marburg 67071

Subjects:

David and musicians

Instrument, reference to—*Seitenspil*

Johannes, Magister (scribe)

Rudolph von Ems [cross-reference to "Ems, Rudolph von"]

Sextet or larger ensemble

Text—Bible—2 Samuel

Text—Biblical adaptation

MS Zurich Zentralbibl Rheinau 15—1
Courtesy of Zentralbibliothek Zürich:
Ms. Rh 15, fol. 218 verso

WORKSHEET

Symbol: NiccolòV School—2   Repro.: P

Artist: School of Niccolò da Varallo

Date/School: Ca. 1460, Italian: Milan

Title: Wedding banquet of Griselda

Medium: Painting: Wall (fresco)   Size:

Location: Milan, Castello Sforzesco, Museo d'arte antica

Description:

The scene depicts the wedding banquet of the patient Griselda and Gualtieri, marchese di Saluzzo (see Boccaccio, *Decameron* X, 10: "Novella di Griselda"). The table is filled with people and more stand behind. Music is supplied by four men playing (1) two *straight trumpets* (with banners); and (2) two *shawms* (one with fontanelle).

The fresco was painted in the Castello di Roccabianca (between Parma and Cremona) for Pier Maria Rossi (condottiere in the service of the Sforzas and the Visconti) for his friend Bianca Pellegrini d'Arluno.

Bibl.: *LorenziAR, p. 8

Subjects:

    Boccaccio: *Decameron*

    Griselda

    Gualtieri, marchese di Saluzzo [cross-reference to "Saluzzo, Gualtieri, marchese di"]

    Meal, music at

    Minstrel

    Pellegrini d'Arluno, Bianca [cross-reference to "Arluno, Bianca Pellegrini d'"]

    Quartet

    Roccabianca, Castello di

    Rossi, Pier Maria

    Text, literary—Short tales

    Wedding celebration, music at

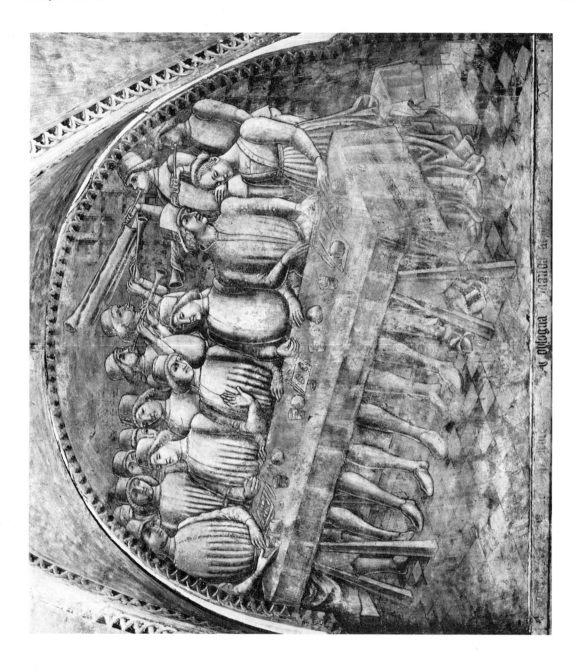

Niccolò V School—-2
Courtesy of Museo d'Arte Antica, Castello Sforzesco

WORKSHEET

Symbol: Painting French 16th c.—2   Repro.: P

Artist: Anon.

Date/School: Ca. 1530, French

Title: Rejoicing of the Jews in Jerusalem

Medium: Painting: Panel   Size:

Location: Rheims, Hôtel—Dieu (Musée de la Ville)

Description:

In a street of Jerusalem, with the Temple of Solomon in the background, the Jews hold an outdoor celebration. In the left foreground, 10 people dance in a circle. The music is supplied by 4 men standing on a platform, playing (1) *folded trumpet*; (2) *unclear wind* (= *shawm*?); (3) *unclear bowed string* (= *fiddle* or *violin*?); and (4) *pipe and tabor.*

According to Paris(L)TP, p. 61, the scene was suggested by the *Mystère de la Vengeance de Jesus-Christ,* performed in Rheims in 1531, and, indeed, the painted canvas may have been used as a backdrop for that production.

Bibl.: *PhotoGiraudon G 37460-61; ThibaultCI, opp. p. 203; DecugisD, pl. 36

Subjects:
    Dancing, round
    Jerusalem
    Jewish music
    Minstrel
    Mystère de la Vengeance de Jesus-Christ
    Platform, musician on
    Quartet
    Rheims
    Text, literary—Drama

Painting French 16th c.—2
Courtesy of Giraudon

WORKSHEET

Symbol: Painting Hellenistic/Roman 3rd/2nd c. B.C.—1   Repro.: X

Artist: Anon. Greek (According to GoodenoughJ I, 63-70, perhaps an Alexandrian)

Date/School: 3rd/2nd c. B.C., Hellenistic in Palestine

Title: Marisa Tomb II: Musicians

Medium: Painting: Wall (Hellenistic Jewish tomb)   Size:

Location: Israel, Marisa (Marîshah), Tomb II

Description:

On the left side of the door to the central burial chamber a woman playing (1) an *arched harp* (5 visible strings) follows a man playing (2) a *double aulos/tibia* down an incline toward the door.

GoodenoughJ I, 71: "The musical approach to the lower world recalls Orpheus and Eurydice, but the identification here can by no means be pressed."

Bibl.: *GoodenoughJ III, 14

Subjects:

Duet

Jewish music (?)

Mythological figure, anon. (?)

Orpheus and Eurydice (?)

Procession

Painting Hellenistic/Roman 3rd/2nd c. B.C.—1

WORKSHEET

Symbol: PfisterVH (1462)—2   Repro.: P

Artist: Anon.

Date/School: 1462, German

Title: *Vier Historien* (Bamberg: Albrecht Pfister, 1462), fol. 46: The Jews Rejoice
   over Judith's Victory

Medium: Print: Woodcut   Size:

Location: Paris BN; Manchester, John Rylands Library

Description:

   The four *Historien* are those of Joseph, Daniel, Esther, and Judith. The scene
illustrates the text: "und opferten got nach moyses gepot ganz enzuntes opfer und
prachten in gabe zu dem tempel" (Apocrypha: Judith).

   The scene shows a group of 6 men offering an animal at an altar. To the right stand
3 men playing (1) *portative organ* (7 pipes in each of 2 rows); (2) *frame harp* (7 strings
but 13 pegs); and (3) *shawm* (5 fingerholes visible; = *unclear conical wind*).

Bibl.: *SchrammDA, pl. 23, fig. 153

Subjects:
   Ceremony, religious—Judaeo-Christian
   Pfister, Albrecht (publisher/printer)
   Text—Bible—Judith (Apocrypha)
   Trio

PfisterVH (1462)—2
Reproduced from Schramm, Bilderschmuck der Frühdrucke Vol. 1 (1922)
with permission of the pubisher Anton Hiersemann, Stuttgart

WORKSHEET

Symbol: Sculpture Exeter—6(a-h)   Repro.: P

Artist: Anon.

Date/School: Ca. 1419, English

Title: Tomb of Bishop Walter Bronescomb

Medium: Sculpture: Monument, sepulchral   Size:

Location: Exeter Cath

Description:

   A stone canopy surmounts the tomb of Walter Bronescomb, Bishop of Exeter (1258-1281). The canopy was probably erected in 1419 on the death of Bishop Edmund Stafford whose tomb adjoins Bronescomb's.

   Running around the top edge of the canopy are small bas reliefs of angels, including 8 angel musicians, who play (a) *portative organ* (ca. 5 pipes in each of three rows); (b) *shawm*; (c) *rebec*; (d) *bagpipe* (1 conical chanter and 1 conical drone); (e) *small lute* (plectrum?); (f) *frame harp*; (g) *incurved trapezoidal psaltery*; and (h) *incurved demi-trapezoidal psaltery* (or *frame harp* or *harp-psaltery*?).

Bibl.: KingH I, pp. 176-77 (no ill.)

Subjects:
   Angel musician
   Bronescomb, Walter, Bishop of Exeter [cross-reference to "Exeter"]
   Sextet or larger ensemble
   Solo musician [each angel alone]

Sculpture Exeter—6 (a-h)
By kind permission of the Dean and Chapter
of Exeter Cathedral   *See next eight pages for details.*

a

b

c

d

e

f

g

h

WORKSHEET

Symbol: Sculpture Franco/Flemish 15th c.—1a-b   Repro.: P

Artist: Anon.

Date/School: 15th c., Franco/Flemish

Title: Chessboard and (on reverse) backgammon board—Scenes of courtly life

Medium: Sculpture—Furniture, secular   Size:

Location: Florence, Museo nazionale (Bargello)

Description:

Each border of both sides of the game boards is decorated with scenes of courtly life.

(a) Chessboard: One border shows 5 men and a woman in Turkish dress. Two of the men have swords and dance to (1) a *pipe and tabor*, while a fool looks on. Perhaps they are dancing a moresca or sword dance.

One border shows knights at a joust.

One border shows three couples dancing, accompanied by four men playing: (2-4) 3 *shawms* of various sizes (1 with fontanelle); and (5) a *folded trumpet*.

One border shows various couples walking and eating.

(b) Backgammon board: The borders shows courtiers hawking, fishing, hunting, etc.

One panel shows a musical couple outdoors; he plays (6) a *shawm* or *recorder* (= *unclear conical wind*), and she plays (7) a *frame harp* (ca. 10 strings).

Another border shows a hunting scene with two men (one mounted) playing (8-9) 2 *curved horns*.

Bibl.: *Alinari photo 2793-2794

Subjects:

Court, music at
Dancing, couple
Dancing—Moresque
Dancing—Sword dance
Duet
Hunting
Informal music-making outdoors
Masquerade
Minstrel
Musical couple
Musician, mounted
Quartet
Solo musician

Sculpture Franco/Flemish 15th c.—1a
Alinari photo

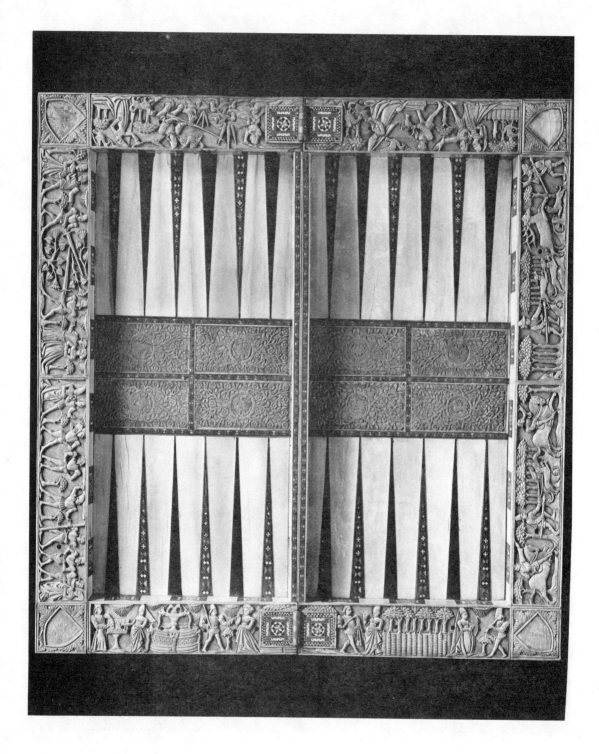

Sculpture Franco/Flemish 15th c.—1b

WORKSHEET

Symbol: Sculpture Hellenistic/Roman 2nd c.—7   Repro.: X

Artist: Anon.

Date/School: 2nd c., Roman

Title: Sarcophagus—Contest between the Muses and the Sirens

Medium: Sculpture—Monument, sepulchral   Size: H.: 1' 9 3/4" (55.2 cm.)

Location: New York, Metropolitan Museum of Art, No. 10.104

Description:

On the left are the Capitoline gods who judge the contest between the Muses (agents of divine inspiration) and the Sirens (agents of human knowledge). One Siren plays (1) a *double aulos/tibia* (?), and another (2) a *lyre/kithara* (plectrum). One of the Muses plays (3) a *lyre/kithara* (plectrum).

On the right the victorious Muses chastise the Sirens.

Bibl.: *PijoanA, p. 379; NewYorkMetCatRA, pl. 10

Subjects:
  Contest, musical
  Duet
  Muses
  Siren
  Solo musician
  Trio

Sculpture Hellenistic/Roman 2nd c.—7
Courtesy of The Metropolitan Museum of Art

WORKSHEET

Symbol: Zavattari—2   Repro.: B; X

Artist: Francesco Zavattari and his sons, Ambrogio and Gregorio

Date/School: 1444, Italian: Lombardy

Title: Legend of Queen Theodolinda—Wedding and Wedding Banquet

Medium: Painting—Wall (fresco)   Size:

Location: Monza (near Milan), Cathedral (Basilica di San Giovanni)

Description:

On the left, the wedding of Theodolinda, Queen of the Lombards, and Agilulf, Duke of Turin, is being celebrated before a Gothic loggia. Music is supplied by two men playing (1-2) long *straight trumpets* (with banners).

On the right, five people are seated at a banquet table. Two servants stand in front of the table. To the left stand three men: one plays (3) a *nonwaisted fiddle* (neck and pegholder not visible; no strings drawn in); the second (4) a *portative organ* (two rows each with about 10 pipes); and the third holds a plectrum in his right hand (his left side is not visible) and must therefore play (5) an *unclear plucked string*.

In the background, two musicians play (6-7) two *folded trumpets* (with banners).

Bibl.: *Photo Alinari 18429; *LeviPisetzkySC II, pl. 220; *Time*, April 14, 1961 [c]; *BerensonCINIS II, pl. 547; *NegriZ, p. 32[c], p. 70

Subjects:

Agilulf, Duke of Turin [cross-reference to "Turin, Agilulf, Duke of"]

Court, music at

Duet

Meal, music at

Minstrel

Quintet

Theodolinda, Queen of the Lombards [cross-reference to "Lombards, Theodolinda, Queen of"]

Trio

Wedding celebration, music at

Zavattari—2
Alinari photo

3. Bibliography of works consulted in preparing appendix A

BerensonCINIS   Bernard Berenson. *Italian Pictures of the Renais-
                                  sance: Central Italian and North Italian Schools.*
                                  Rev. ed. by Luisa Vertova. 3 vols. London:
                                  Phaidon, 1968.
ClevelandMABull   *Bulletin of the Cleveland Museum of Art*
ClevelandMACatGA   Cleveland Museum of Art. *Gothic Art 1360-
                                  1440: An Introduction to the Gotha Missa* [by
                                  William D. Wixom] *and a Catalogue to the Exhi-
                                  bition . . . Held at The Cleveland Museum of Art,
                                  August 8 through September 15, 1963.* Cleve-
                                  land, 1963.
ClevelandMACatH(1966)   Cleveland Museum of Art. *Handbook.* Cleveland,
                                  1966.
DecugisD   Nicole Decugis and Suzanne Reymond. *Le Décor
                                  de théâtre en France du moyen âge à 1925.* Paris:
                                  Compagnie française des arts graphiques, 1953.
DeWaldUP   E. T. DeWald. *The Illustrations of the Utrecht
                                  Psalter.* Princeton: Princeton University Press,
                                  [1932].
EgbertTP   Donald Drew Egbert. *The Tickhill Psalter and
                                  Related Manuscripts.* New York: The New York
                                  Public Library and the Department of Art and
                                  Archeology of Princeton University. 1940.
EngelbregtUP   J. H. A. Engelbregt. *Het Utrechts Psalterium:
                                  Een Eeuw Wetenschappelijke Bestudering (1860-
                                  1960).* Utrecht: Haentjens Dekker and Gumbert,
                                  1965.
FreyhanIC   Robert Freyhan. *Die Illustrationen zum Casseler
                                  Willehalm-Codex.* Marburg: Verlag des Kunst-
                                  geschictlichen Seminars, 1927.
GoodenoughJ   Erwin R. Goodenough. *Jewish Symbols in the
                                  Greco-Roman Period.* 12 vols. New York:
                                  Pantheon Books, n.d.
HoytWP   Anna C. Hoyt. "The Woodcuts of the Planets
                                  Formerly Attributed to Hans Sebald Beham."
                                  In *Boston Museum of Fine Arts Bulletin* 52
                                  (1954): 2-10.
HutterM   Heribert Hutter. *Medieval Stained Glass.* Trans-
                                  lated by Margaret Shenfield. New York: Crown
                                  Publishers, 1964.
KarlingerK   Hans Karlinger. *Die Kunst Der Gotik.* Berlin:
                                  Propyläen-Verlag, 1927.

KingH — [Richard John King.] *Handbook to the Cathedrals of England.* Part I: *Winchester-Salisbury-Exeter-Wells.* London: J. Murray, 1861.

LesureD — François Lesure. "Danses et chansons à danser au début du XVIe siècle." In *Recueil de travaux offert à M. Clovis Brunel* (Paris: Société de l'École des Chartes, 1955), pp. 176-184.

LeviPisetzkySC — Rosita Levi Pisetzky. *Storia del Costume in Italia.* 2 vols. Milan: Istituto editoriale italiano, 1964.

LorenziAR — Alberto Lorenzi. *Gli Affreschi di Roccabianca.* Milan: Museo d'arte antica al Castello Sforzesco, 1967.

MalletJP — Robert Mallet. *Jardins et Paradis.* Paris: Gallimard, 1959.

NegriZ — Renata Negri. *Gli Zavattari: La Cappella di Teodolinda.* Milan: Fabbri and Skira, 1965.

NewYorkMetCatGM — New York, The Metropolitan Museum of Art. *Greek Mythology,* by Roberta Paine. New York, n.d.

NewYorkMetCatRA — New York, The Metropolitan Museum of Art. *Roman Art,* by Christine Alexander. New York, 1936.

PalUP — Paleographical Society. *The Latin Psalter in the University Library of Utrecht.* London: Spencer, Sawyer, Bird and Co., [1874].

ParisBNCatRothschild — Émile Picot. *Catalogue des livres composant la bibliothèque de feu M. le baron James de Rothschild.* 5 vols. Paris: D. Morgand, 1884-1920.

Paris(L)TP — Louis Paris. *Toiles peintes et tapisseries de la ville de Reims.* Rheims: H. de Bruslart, 1843.

PijoanA — Joseph Pijoan. *Art in Ancient Times.* Chicago: University of Knowledge, 1940.

SchrammDA — Albert Schramm. *Die Drucke von Albrecht Pfister in Bamberg.* Leipzig: K. W. Hiersemann, 1922.

ThibaultCI — G. Thibault. "Le concert instrumental dans l'art flamand au XVe siècle et au début du XVIe." In *La Renaissance dans les provinces du Nord,* ed. François Lesure. Paris: Centre national de la recherche scientifique, 1956, pp. 197-206.

ToescaTS — Elena Berti Toesca. *Il Tacuinum Sanitatis della Biblioteca Nazionale di Parigi.* Bergamo: Istituto italiano d'arti grafiche editore, 1936.

UnescoCat

VieNNaNBCatIH V2

WinternitzMI

YatesVT

ZurichSM

The UNESCO Catalogue of Colour Reproductions of Paintings Prior to 1860. New York: UNESCO, 1962.

Die illuminierten Handschriften und Inkunablen der Nationalbibliothek in Wien, ed. Julius Schlosser and Hermann Julius Hermann. Leipzig: K. W. Hiersemann, 1923-1938. Vol. V/2: *Die italienischen Handschriften des Dugento und Trecento,* by Hermann Julius Hermann. 1929.

Emanuel Winternitz. *Musical Instruments and Their Symbolism in Western Art.* New York: W. W. Norton, 1967.

Frances A. Yates. *The Valois Tapestries.* London: Warburg Institute, 1959.

Schätze aus Museen und Sammlungen in Zürich. Zurich, 1968.

4. Sample cards from the cross-reference files

As explained in chapter II, the information about each work of art gathered on the central card or worksheet is divided into various categories, which are then isolated in a series of six cross-reference files. Appendix A, section 3 above, for example, explains all of the sigla used as bibliographical references in appendix A. The other kinds of information, the school and date of the work of art, its medium or type, its present location, the instruments pictured, and the subject entries, are gathered and listed by century in a series of cross-reference files kept on 4 by 6 cards. To illustrate this procedure samples of the cards prepared from the material in appendix A are shown in the following pages. Thus, for the cross-reference file of schools and dates, the four sixteenth-century French examples are listed on one card and the two fourteenth-century German ones on another; for the cross-reference file of present locations, the four objects in the Bibliothèque Nationale are separated from the two in the Cleveland Museum of Art. And a separate card lists all examples from one century of each subject entry; I have arbitrarily chosen "Quartet" to illustrate the procedure.

A. Sample cards from the cross-reference file of schools and dates

French — 16th c.

    Basses dances (n.d.)—1
    Caron—1
    DoratMS (1573)—1
    Painting French 16th c.—2

Germanic: German — 14th c.

    MS Cassel LB poet. et rom. fol. 1—2
    MS Zurich Zentralbibl Rheinau 15—1

B. Sample cards from the cross-reference file of mediums or types of objects

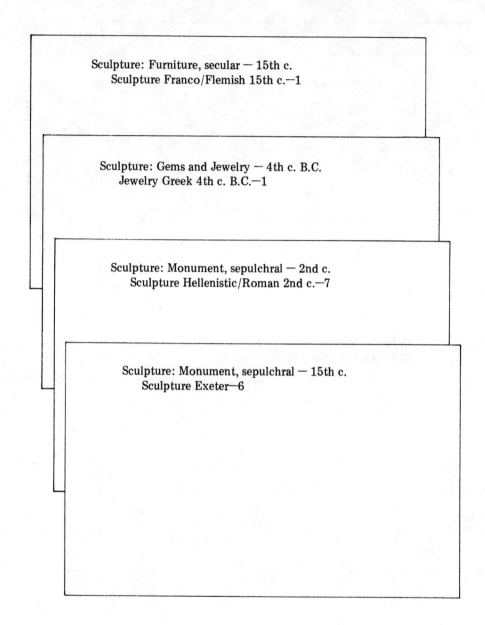

Sculpture: Furniture, secular — 15th c.
Sculpture Franco/Flemish 15th c.—1

Sculpture: Gems and Jewelry — 4th c. B.C.
Jewelry Greek 4th c. B.C.—1

Sculpture: Monument, sepulchral — 2nd c.
Sculpture Hellenistic/Roman 2nd c.—7

Sculpture: Monument, sepulchral — 15th c.
Sculpture Exeter—6

C. Sample cards from the cross-reference file of present locations

Cleveland, Museum of Art

Enamel Italian 14th c.—1
Hooch—3

Paris, Bibliothèque Nationale

Basses dances (n.d.)—1
DoratMS (1573)—1
MS Paris BN nouv. acq. lat. 1673—4
PfisterVH (1462)—2

D. Sample cards from the cross-reference file of instruments pictured

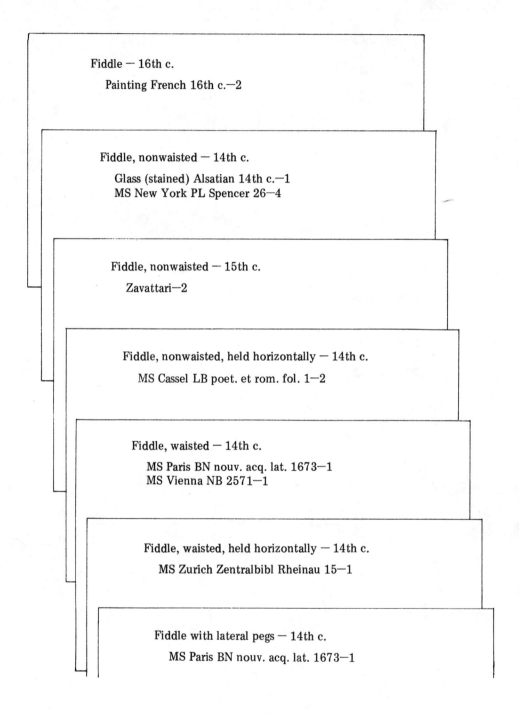

Fiddle — 16th c.

    Painting French 16th c.—2

Fiddle, nonwaisted — 14th c.

    Glass (stained) Alsatian 14th c.—1
    MS New York PL Spencer 26—4

Fiddle, nonwaisted — 15th c.

    Zavattari—2

Fiddle, nonwaisted, held horizontally — 14th c.

    MS Cassel LB poet. et rom. fol. 1—2

Fiddle, waisted — 14th c.

    MS Paris BN nouv. acq. lat. 1673—1
    MS Vienna NB 2571—1

Fiddle, waisted, held horizontally — 14th c.

    MS Zurich Zentralbibl Rheinau 15—1

Fiddle with lateral pegs — 14th c.

    MS Paris BN nouv. acq. lat. 1673—1

E. Sample cards from the cross-reference file of subject entries

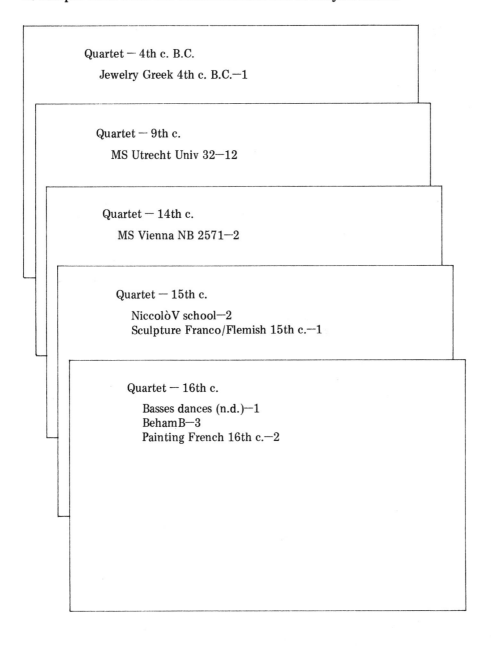

Quartet — 4th c. B.C.
  Jewelry Greek 4th c. B.C.—1

Quartet — 9th c.
  MS Utrecht Univ 32—12

Quartet — 14th c.
  MS Vienna NB 2571—2

Quartet — 15th c.
  NiccolòV school—2
  Sculpture Franco/Flemish 15th c.—1

Quartet — 16th c.
  Basses dances (n.d.)—1
  BehamB—3
  Painting French 16th c.—2

APPENDIX B.
LIST OF MOST COMMON NAMES FOR INSTRUMENTS WITH CROSS REFERENCES

This list includes instrument names used in standard bibliographical sources and anthologies of music in pictures and those used to label instruments in early art sources. It does not include the hundreds of names found in ancient, medieval, Renaissance, and Baroque literary and archival sources; many of these are listed and defined in Sybil Marcuse, *Musical Instruments: A Comprehensive Dictionary* (New York: Doubleday, 1964). For a list of names applied to instruments in pictorial sources before 1800, see "Instrument, reference to," in appendix C.

Ala bohemica. *See* Zither-Ala Bohemica
Angular harp. *See* Harp, angular
Arc musical. *See* Bow, musical
Arc sonore. *See* Bow, musical
Arched harp. *See* Harp, arched
Archlute. *See* Lute, arch-
Archiluth. *See* Lute, arch-
Arciliuto. *See* Lute, arch-
Arco musical. *See* Bow, musical
Arco sonoro. *See* Bow, musical
Arpa. *See* Harp
Arpanetta. *See* Psaltery, double
Aulos/Tibia (single pipe)
Aulos/Tibia, double
Aulos/Tibia, Phrygian
Aulos/Tibia, Phrygian, with rotary rings
Bagpipe. *See also* Bladder pipe
Bajón. *See* Curtal
Bandora; Bandore. *See* Cittern–Bandora/Orpharion
Barrel drum. *See* Drum, barrel
Baryton. *See* Viol–Baryton
Basson. *See* Bassoon; Curtal
Bassoon. *See also* Curtal
Beaten pot. *See* Pot, beaten
Becken. *See* Cymbals

Bell
Bell chime. *See* Bell, clapper–Chime; Bell, struck–Chime
Bell, clapper
Bell, clapper–Chime
Bell, clapper–Hand bell
Bell, pellet
Bell, struck
Bell, struck–Chime
Bladder pipe, curved. *See also* Bagpipe; Crumhorn
Bladder pipe, straight. *See also* Bagpipe
Blockflöte. *See* Flute, fipple–Recorder; Pipe and tabor
Bogenharfe. *See* Harp, arched
Bohemian wing. *See* Zither–Ala bohemica
Boîte à musique. *See* Mechanical instrument
Bombard; Bombarde; Bombardt. *See* Shawm
Bow, musical
Bratsche. *See* Violin–Viola
Buisine. *See* Horn, curved; Trumpet, straight
Busaun. *See* Trombone
Busîne; Buzine. *See* Horn, curved; Trumpet, straight
Campana. *See* Bell
Cariglione. *See* Bell, clapper–Chime; Bell, struck–Chime
Carillon. *See* Bell, clapper–Chime; Bell, struck–Chime
Carnyx. *See* Trumpet, hooked–Carnyx
Castanets. *See* Clappers
Cello. *See* Violoncello
Cembalo. *See* Harpsichord
Cembalo verticale. *See* Clavicytherium
Cervelas; Cervelat. *See* Racket
Cetera. *See* Cittern
Chalemie. *See* Shawm
Chalumeau. [*See* XIV.3.b above]
Chifonie. *See* Organistrum
Chime; Chime bell. *See* Bell, clapper–Chime; Bell, struck–Chime
Chirimía. *See* Shawm
Chitarra. *See* Guitar
Chitarrone. *See* Lute, arch-
Chofar. *See* Horn, curved
Chorus. *See* "Instrument, reference to–*Chorus*" in appendix C
Chrotta. *See* Harp; Lyre, northern; Zither
Cinelli. *See* Cymbals
Cister; Cistre. *See* Cittern
Cithara. *See* Lyre/Kithara
Citole. *See* Cittern; Guitar
Cittern
Cittern–Bandora/Orpharion
Clapper bell. *See* Bell, clapper

Clapper bell chime. *See* Bell, clapper– Chime
Clappers
Clappers, foot
Clappers, rectangular
Clappers, round
Clappers, round, on sticks
Clarion. *See* Trumpet, folded; Trumpet, straight
Clavecin. *See* Harpsichord
Clavecin organisé. *See* Claviorganum
Clavecin, vertical. *See* Clavicytherium
Clavicembalo. *See* Harpsichord
Clavichord
Clavicorde; Clavicordio. *See* Clavichord
Clavicytherium
Clavicytherium, portative
Claviorgano. *See* Claviorganum
Claviorganum
Cleron. *See* Trumpet
Cliquet; Cliquette. *See* Clappers
Cloche. *See* Bell
Clochettes. *See* Bell, clapper–Chime; Bell, struck–Chime
Colachon. *See* Lute, long
Colascione. *See* Lute, long
Contrabasso. *See* Violone
Contrebasse. *See* Violone
Cor. *See* Horn
Cor de chasse. *See* Horn, coiled; Horn, curved; Horn, S-shaped
Cornemuse. *See* Bagpipe; Bagpipe, bellows-blown
Cornet à bouquin. *See* Cornett
Cornet courbe. *See* Cornett, S-shaped
Cornet droit. *See* Cornett, straight
Corneta. *See* Cornett
Corneta tuerta. *See* Cornett, S-shaped
Cornett, curved
Cornett, mute. *See* Cornett, straight
Cornett–Serpent
Cornett, S-shaped
Cornett, straight
Cornetto. *See* Cornett
Cornetto curvo. *See* Cornett, S-shaped
Cornetto dritto. *See* Cornett, straight
Corno. *See* Horn
Corno da caccia. *See* Horn, coiled; Horn, curved; Horn, S-shaped
Corno torto. *See* Cornett, S-shaped
Cornu. *See* Trumpet, G-shaped–Cornu
Cortali. *See* Racket
Cromorne. *See* Crumhorn

Cross flute. *See* Flute, transverse
Crot. *See* Harp; Lyre, northern; Zither
Crotal. *See* Clappers, round, on sticks
Crowd. *See* Harp; Lyre, northern; Zither
Cruit. *See* Harp; Lyre, northern; Zither
Crumhorn. *See also* Bladder pipe, curved
Crwth. *See* Harp; Lyre, northern; Zither
Curtal
Cylindrical drum. *See* Drum, cylindrical
Cymbal. *See* Cymbals
Cymbala. *See* Bell, clapper–Chime; Bell, struck–Chime
Cymbales. *See* Cymbals
Cymbals
Cymbals played with vertical motion
Cymbals struck with stick (includes gongs)
Diaulos. *See* Aulos/Tibia, double
Dolcian. *See* Curtal
Double bass. *See* Violone
Drum. *See also* Pot, beaten
Drum, barrel
Drum, cylindrical
Drum, cylindrical, with pipe. *See* Pipe and tabor
Drum, cylindrical, with snare
Drum, frame
Drum, frame–Tambourine
Drum, friction
Drum, kettle
Drum, string. *See* Zither–Scheitholt
Dudelsack. *See* Bagpipe
Dulcimer. *See* Psaltery, struck
Dulzian. *See* Curtal
Épinette. *See* Spinet
Erzlaute. *See* Lute, arch-
Fagot; Fagote; Fagott; Fagotto. *See* Bassoon; Curtal
Fasstrommel. *See* Drum, barrel
Felttrumet. *See* Trumpet
Fiddle, bass. *See* Violone
Fiddle, keyed
Fiddle, nonwaisted
Fiddle, nonwaisted, held horizontally
Fiddle, nonwaisted, held upright
Fiddle, plucked. *See* Guitar
Fiddle, pocket
Fiddle, waisted
Fiddle, waisted, held horizontally
Fiddle, waisted, held upright
Fiddle with drone strong (list in addition to other fiddle categories)

Fiddle with lateral pegs (list in addition to other fiddle categories)

Fiedel. *See* Fiddle

Fife. *See* Flute, transverse

Fiffaro. *See* Flute, transverse

Fifre. *See* Flute, transverse

Fipple flute. *See* Flute, fipple

Flageol. *See* Flute, fipple; Recorder; Pipe and tabor

Flageolet. *See* Flute, fipple–Recorder; Pipe and tabor

Flauta. *See* Flute

Flauta de pico. *See* Flute, fipple–Recorder; Pipe and tabor

Flauto. *See* Flute

Flauto di Pan. *See* Flute–Panpipes

Flauto dritto. *See* Flute, fipple–Recorder

Flauto traverso. *See* Flute, transverse

Flötenuhr. *See* Mechanical instrument–Musical clock

Flûte à bec. *See* Flute, fipple–Recorder

Flûte à bloc. *See* Flute, fipple

Flûte de Pan. *See* Flute–Panpipes

Flute, fipple–Recorder

Flute, fipple–Recorder, double

Flute, fipple–Tabor pipe. *See* Pipe and tabor

Flute–Panpipes, bowl-shaped

Flute–Panpipes, raft-shaped

Flute–Panpipes, rectangular

Flute polycalame. *See* Flute–Panpipes

Flute, prehistoric

Flute, transverse

Flûte traversière. *See* Flute, transverse

Foot clappers. *See* Clappers, foot

Frame drum. *See* Drum, frame

Frame harp. *See* Harp, frame

French horn. *See* Horn, coiled

Friction drum. *See* Drum, friction

Gamba. *See* Viol

Geige. *See* Fiddle; Rebec; Violin

Gerader Zink. *See* Cornett, straight

German flute. *See* Flute, transverse

Ghittern. *See* Guitar

Gitarre. *See* Guitar

Gittern. *See* Guitar

Glocke. *See* Bell

Glockenspiel. *See* Bell, clapper–Chime; Bell, struck–Chime

Gong. *See* Cymbals struck with stick

Grelot. *See* Bell, pellet

Guimbarde. *See* Jew's harp

Guitar

Guitar, nonwaisted

Guitar, waisted
Guitar with thumb hole (list in addition to other guitar categories)
Guitar with vaulted back (list in addition to other guitar categories)
Guitare. *See* Guitar
Guitarra. *See* Guitar
Guitarra battente. *See* Guitar with vaulted back
Guiterne. *See* Guitar
Hackbrett. *See* Psaltery, struck
Hand bell. *See* Bell, clapper–Hand bell
Harfe. *See* Harp
Harfenett. *See* Psaltery, double
Harp, angular
Harp, arched
Harp, frame
Harp, frame–Double
Harp, frame–Hook
Harp, frame–Triple
Harp, jaw's; Harp, Jew's. *See* Jew's harp
Harpe à cadre. *See* Harp, frame
Harpe angulaire. *See* Harp, angular
Harpe arquée. *See* Harp, arched
Harpff. *See* Harp
Harp-psaltery. *See* Psaltery, harp-
Harpsichord. *See also* Claviorganum
Harpsichord, double (two manuals)
Harpsichord-and-Organ. *See* Claviorganum
Harpsichord, upright. *See* Clavicytherium
Hautbois. *See* Oboe; Shawm
Horn. *See also* Cornett
Horn, coiled
Horn, curved
Horn, curved–Oliphant
Horn, S-shaped
Horn, straight
Hornpipe
Hornpipe, double
Hrota, Hrotta. *See* Harp; Lyre, northern; Zither
Hunting horn. *See* Horn, coiled; Horn, curved; Horn, S-shaped
Hurdy-gurdy. *See* Organistrum
Hydraulos. *See* Organ, hydraulic
Jagdhorn. *See* Horn, coiled; Horn, curved; Horn, S-shaped
Jägerhorn. *See* Horn, coiled; Horn, curved; Horn, S-shaped
Jaw's harp. *See* Jew's harp
Jew's harp
Karnyx. *See* Trumpet, hooked–Carnyx
Kettledrum. *See* Drum, kettle
Kielflügel. *See* Harpsichord

Kit. *See* Fiddle, pocket; Rebec, pocket; Violin, pocket

Kithara. *See* Lyre/Kithara

Klapper. *See* Clappers

Klavichord. *See* Clavichord

Klavizytherium. *See* Clavicytherium

Kontrabass. *See* Violone

Krotala. *See* Clappers, rectangular

Kroupalon. *See* Clappers, foot

Kroupezion; Krupezion. *See* Clappers, foot

Krummer Zink. *See* Cornett, S-shaped

Krummhorn. *See* Crumhorn

Krupezion. *See* Clappers, foot

Laute. *See* Lute

Lira. *See* Rebec

Lira da braccio. *See* Fiddle, waisted, with drone string

Lituus. *See* Trumpet, hooked–Lituus

Liuto. *See* Lute

Liuto attiorbato. *See* Lute, arch-

Llaviórgano. *See* Claviorganum

Long lute. *See* Lute, long

Lute

Lute, arch- (chitarrone, theorbo, theorboed lute)

Lute, long (colascione)

Lute played left-handed (list in addition to other lute categories)

Lute, theorboed. *See* Lute, arch-

Lute-zither. *See* Zither, lute-

Luth. *See* Lute

Luth théorbé. *See* Lute, arch-

Lyra. *See* Lyre/Kithara

Lyra viol. *See* Viol

Lyre/Kithara

Lyre, northern, nonwaisted

Lyre, northern, waisted

Lyre, northern, bowed–Nonwaisted

Lyre, northern, bowed–Waisted

Lyre, northern, with fingerboard (list in addition to other northern lyre categories)

Mandola. *See* Mandora

Mandora

Mandora–Pandurina

Mandore. *See* Mandora

Maultrommel. *See* Jew's harp

Mechanical instrument

Mechanical instrument–Musical clock

Monaulos. *See* Aulos/Tibia (single pipe)

Monochord

Monocorde; Monocordo. *See* Monochord

Musette. *See* Bagpipe; Bagpipe, bellows-blown

Musical bow. *See* Bow, musical
Musical clock. *See* Mechanical instrument–Musical clock
Musikbogen. *See* Bow, musical
Mute cornett. *See* Cornett, straight
Nacaire. *See* Drum, kettle
Nacara. *See* Drum, kettle
Nacchera. *See* Drum, kettle
Naker. *See* Drum, kettle
Oboe
Olifant. *See* Horn, curved–Oliphant
Oliphant. *See* Horn, curved–Oliphant
Organ, hydraulic
Organ, large (position of keyboards and pipes fixed)
Organ, portative
Organ, positive
Organ, regal
Organ-and-Harpsichord. *See* Claviorganum
Organ-and-Spinet. *See* Claviorganum
Organ-and-Virginal. *See* Claviorganum
Organistrum
Organistrum, nonwaisted. *See also* Organistrum, rectangular
Organistrum, rectangular
Organistrum, two-man (list in addition to other organistrum categories)
Organistrum, waisted
Organo. *See* Organ
Orgel. *See* Organ
Orgelklavier. *See* Claviorganum
Orgue. *See* Organ
Orlo. *See* Crumhorn
Orpharion. *See* Cittern–Bandora/Orpharion
Panderete. *See* Drum, frame–Tambourine
Pandora; Pandore. *See* Cittern–Bandora/Orpharion
Panpipes. *See* Flute–Panpipes
Pauke. *See* Drum, kettle
Pellet bell. *See* Bell, pellet
Pfeiff. *See* Flute, transverse; Flute, fipple–Recorder; etc.
Phrygian auloi. *See* Aulos/Tibia, phrygian
Piatti. *See* Cymbals
Pibcorn; Pibgorn. *See* Hornpipe
Pífano. *See* Flute, transverse
Piffaro. *See* Shawm
Pipe. *See* by names of individual wind instruments
Pipe and tabor
Pipe and tabor–Pipe alone
Pipe and tabor with snare
Pipe, bladder. *See* Bladder pipe
Pipe, tabor. *See* Pipe and tabor

Piva torto. *See* Crumhorn

Platerspiel; Platerspil. *See* Bladder pipe

Poche; Pochette. *See* Fiddle, pocket; Rebec, pocket; Violin, pocket

Pommer. *See* Shawm

Portativ. *See* Organ, portative

Posaune. *See* Trombone

Positif; Positiff. *See* Organ, positive

Positiv. *See* Organ, positive

Pot, beaten

Psaltérion. *See* Psaltery

Psalterium. *See* Psaltery

Psaltery

Psaltery, demi-trapezoidal

Psaltery, double

Psaltery, harp-

Psaltery, incurved demi-trapezoidal

Psaltery, incurved trapezoidal

Psaltery, rectangular

Psaltery, square

Psaltery, struck (list in addition to other psaltery categories)

Psaltery, trapezoidal

Psaltery, triangular

Pseudo-instrument. *See* "Instrument, pseudo-" in appendix C

Querflöte. *See* Flute, transverse

Querpfeife. *See* Flute, transverse

Rabel. *See* Rebec

Racket

Racket–Tartold

Rahmenharfe. *See* Harp, frame

Rahmentrommel. *See* Drum, frame

Rankett. *See* Racket

Rattle, cog

Rattle, frame

Rattle, pendant

Rattle, sliding

Rattle, stick

Rattle, suspension

Rattle, vessel. *See also* Bell, pellet

Rauschpfeife. *See* Shawm, reed-capped

Realejo. *See* Organ, regal

Rebec

Rebec bowed left-handed (list in addition to other rebec categories)

Rebec, pocket

Recorder. *See* Flute, fipple–Recorder

Reed-capped instrument. *See* Crumhorn; Shawm, reed-capped

Reedpipe (ancient). *See* Aulos/Tibia

Reedpipe (medieval, Renaissance, Baroque). *See* Bagpipe; Bassoon; Bladder pipe;
   Crumhorn; Hornpipe; Oboe; Racket; Shawm

Regal; Régale. *See* Organ, regal
Reibtrommel. *See* Drum, friction
Ribeca. *See* Rebec
Röhrentrommel. *See* Drum, cylindrical
Rommelpot. *See* Drum, friction
Rota; Rote; Rotta; Rotte. *See* Harp; Lyre, northern; Zither
Rummelpot. *See* Drum, friction
Sackbut. *See* Trombone
Sackpfeife. *See* Bagpipe
Sambuca; Sambyke. *See* Harp (ancient Greek and Roman)
Scacciapensieri. *See* Jew's harp
Schalmei; Schalmey. *See* Shawm
Scheidtholtt. *See* Zither—Scheitholt
Scheitholt. *See* Zither–Scheitholt
Schelle. *See* Bell
Schellentrommel. *See* Drum, frame–Tambourine
Schlangenrohr. *See* Cornett–Serpent
Schlüsselfiedel. *See* Fiddle, keyed
Schofar. *See* Horn, curved
Schwegel. *See* Flute, transverse; Pipe and tabor
Serpent. *See* Cornett–Serpent
Serpentón; Serpentone. *See* Cornett–Serpent
Shawm
Shawm, double
Shawm, reed-capped
Shofar. *See* Horn, curved
Sifflet de Pan. *See* Flute–Panpipes
Siringa. *See* Flute–Panpipes
Sistro. *See* Rattle, stick
Sistrum. *See* Rattle, stick
Sordino. *See* Fiddle, pocket; Rebec, pocket; Violin, pocket
Sourdeline. *See* Bagpipe, bellows-blown
Snare drum. *See* Drum, cylindrical, with snare
Spinet. *See also* Claviorganum; Virginal
Spinet-and-Organ. *See* Claviorganum
Spinett; Spinetta. *See* Spinet
Spitzharfe. *See* Psaltery, double
Storto. *See* Crumhorn
String drum. *See* Zither–Scheitholt
Struck bell. *See* Bell, struck
Struck cymbals. *See* Cymbals struck with stick
Struck psaltery. *See* Psaltery, struck
Surdelina. *See* Bagpipe, bellows-blown
Symphonie. *See* Organistrum
Syrinx. *See* Flute–Panpipes (ancient)
Tabor. *See* Drum; Pipe and tabor
Tabor pipe. *See* Pipe and tabor
Tambor de fricción. *See* Drum, friction

Tambour. *See* Drum
Tambour à friction. *See* Drum, friction
Tambour en cylindre. *See* Drum, cylindrical
Tambour en tonneau. *See* Drum, barrel
Tambour sur cadre. *See* Drum, frame
Tambourin à cordes. *See* Zither–Scheitholt
Tambourine. *See* Drum, frame–Tambourine
Tamburin. *See* Drum, frame–Tambourine
Tamburino. *See* Drum, frame–Tambourine
Tamburo. *See* Drum
Tarrena. *See* Clappers
Tartold; Tartoelt. *See* Racket–Tartold
Taschengeige. *See* Fiddle, pocket; Rebec, pocket; Violin, pocket
Théorbe. *See* Lute, arch-
Theorbenlaute. *See* Lute, arch-
Theorbierte Laute. *See* Lute, arch-
Theorbo. *See* Lute, arch-
Theorboed lute. *See* Lute, arch-
Three-holed pipe. *See* Pipe and tabor
Thurnerhorn. *See* Horn
Tibia. *See* Aulos/Tibia
Tibiae phrygiae. *See* Aulos/Tibia, Phrygian
Timbale. *See* Drum, kettle
Timbrel. *See* Drum, frame–Tambourine
Timpano. *See* Drum, kettle
Tiorba; Tiorbato. *See* Lute, arch-
Tournebout. *See* Crumhorn
Transverse flute. *See* Flute, transverse
Traversière. *See* Flute, transverse
Triangel. *See* Triangle
Triangle
Triangle with jingles
Triangolo. *See* Triangle
Tricca-vallacca. *See* Rattle, frame
Tricche-ballache. *See* Rattle, frame
Trigonon. *See* Harp; Psaltery [in ancient Greek art]
Tromba. *See* Trumpet
Tromba marine. *See* Trumpet marine
Trombone. *See also* Trumpet, slide
Trommel. *See* Drum
Trommelpfeife. *See* Pipe and tabor
Trompa. *See* Horn
Trompe de chasse. *See* Horn, coiled; Horn, curved; Horn, S-shaped
Trompete; Trompette. *See* Trumpet
Trompette marine. *See* Trumpet marine
Trumpet, animal-headed. *See* Trumpet, hooked–Carnyx
Trumpet, conical, curved

Trumpet, conical, straight
Trumpet, curved
Trumpet, folded. *See also* Trumpet, S-shaped
Trumpet, G-shaped–Cornu
Trumpet, hooked
Trumpet, hooked–Carnyx
Trumpet, hooked–Lituus
Trumpet, marine
Trumpet, slide. *See also* Trombone
Trumpet, S-shaped
Trumpet, straight
Trumscheit. *See* Trumpet marine
Tuba. *See* Trumpet, straight (ancient)
Tympani. *See* Drum, kettle
Tympanon. *See* Drum, frame (ancient Greek and Roman); Psaltery, struck
Tympanum. *See* Drum, frame (ancient Greek and Roman)
Unclear instrument
Unclear keyboard
Unclear percussion
Unclear string
Unclear string, bowed
Unclear string, held upright (list in addition to other categories)
Unclear string, played left-handed (list in addition to other categories)
Unclear string, plucked
Unclear wind
Unclear wind, conical
Unclear wind, conical, double
Unclear wind, conical, S-shaped
Unclear wind, cylindrical
Unclear wind, cylindrical, double
Vèze. *See* Bladder pipe; Bagpipe
Vièle. *See* Fiddle
Vièle à roue. *See* Organistrum
Vièlle. *See* Fiddle
Vihuela. *See* Guitar in Spanish art work
Viol
Viol–Baryton
Viol, double bass. *See* Violone
Viola. *See* Violin–Viola
Viola bastarda. *See* Viol
Viola da braccio. *See* Fiddle; Violin
Viola da gamba. *See* Viol
Viola di bordone. *See* Viol–Baryton
Violin. *See also* Fiddle with lateral pegs
Violin, pocket
Violin–Viola
Violine, Violino. *See* Violin
Violon. *See* Violin

Violoncelle. *See* Violoncello

Violoncello

Violone (double bass and double bass viol with player standing) For viol with player
   seated, *see* Viol

Virginal. *See also* Claviorganum; Spinet

Virginal, double

Virginal-and-Organ. *See* Claviorganum

Walzentrommel. *See* Drum, cylindrical

Wasserorgel. *See* Organ, hydraulic

Whistle. *See* Flute

Winkelharfe. *See* Harp, angular

Xylophone

Zink. *See* Cornett

Zither. *See also* Psaltery

Zither–Ala bohemica

Zither, lute-

Zither, nonwaisted

Zither–Scheitholt

Zither, waisted

Zwerchpfeiff. *See* Flute, transverse

APPENDIX C.
SUBJECT ENTRIES GATHERED TO DATE

The following list of subject entries is merely a compilation of items already collected for the Index of Musical Iconography. It is presented here not as a comprehensive list, but only to demonstrate the kinds of information that must be gathered in order to use pictorial sources as musicological evidence. The techniques of determining subject entries are explained in chapter XIII above.

Aaron, Piero
Abraham
Abraham and Melchizedek
Abraham, History of, Tapestries. *See* Tapestries, History of Abraham
Abundance personified
Academy, music at (musical scenes at 16th- and 17-century academies [mainly Italian]; usually musicians are shown singing or playing around a table [no food or drink on table]). *See also* Meistersinger
Achilles
Achillini, J. Philoteus
Acrobat or juggler
Acrobat or juggler musician
Actaeon
Actor musician. *See also* Komast; Theatrical spectacle with music
Acts, Book of. *See* Text–Bible–Acts
Adam and Eve
Adder. *See* Aspis and music
Adimari, Boccaccio
Adimari Cassone. *See* Cassone, Adimari
Admetus
Adoration of the Magi. *See* Christ–Adoration of the Magi
Adoration of the Shepherds. *See* Christ–Adoration of the Shepherds
Aeman. *See* Heman
Aeneid. See Virgil—*Aeneid*
Aesop
Aethan. *See* Ethan
Ages of man
Ages of man–Childhood
Ages of man–Maturity
Ages of man–Old age

Ages of woman. *See* Ages of man
Agilulf, Duke of Turin
Aglaia. *See* Graces, Three
Agnello, Messer Johanni dell'
Agricola, Martin
Ahasuerus, feast of (Book of Esther)
Albani Psalter. *See* Psalter, St. Albans
Albert. *See* Albrecht
Albrecht IV of Bavaria
Albrecht, Marchschal von Baprechtswile
Aldobrandini, Giacomo di Filippo
Alexander, Der Wilde
Alexander, Romance of. *See* Romance of Alexander
Alexander the Great
Alfonso II, King of Naples
Alfonso Psalter. *See* Psalter, Alfonso
Alison (shepherdess)
Alkaios
Allegory, musical. *See* Instrumentarium, complete; Liberal arts–Music; Mode, church, personified; Music personified; Senses, allegory of–Hearing; Winds, four, personified
Allegory of hearing. *See* Senses, allegory of–Hearing
Allegory of Redemption. *See* Redemption, allegory of
Allegory of Senses. *See* Senses, allegory of
Allegory of virtue and vice. *See* Virtues and vices personified
Alma redemptoris mater. *See* Mass and Office–Antiphon, Marian–Alma redemptoris mater
Almanac. *See* Text, didactic–Calendar
Aloris (shepherdess)
Alphonse, Psalter of. *See* Psalter, Alfonso
Altar. *See* altars by name, e.g., Altar, Ghent; Altar–Malvagna Triptych
Altar–Donne Triptych
Altar, Essener
Altar, Ghent
Altar, Grabower
Altar, Isenheim
Altar, Kreuz
Altar–Malvagna Triptych
Altar, Rügenwalder Silber-
Altar, St. Wolfgang
Altar, Weltgerichts-
Altar, Xantener
Amateur musician. *See* Informal music-making
Ambassadors, The
Ameto. *See* Boccaccio–Ameto
Ammerbach, Elias Nicolaus
Amphion
Ananias
Andes (Roman trumpeter)
Andromeda y Perseo Fabula. *See* Opera–Andromeda y Perseo Fabula
Angel musician. *See also* Putto musician; Putto musician, winged
Angel musician, wingless

Angelrot, Balthasar
Angelus, Johannes
Animal musician
Animal musician–Ape
> Bear
> Cat
> Donkey
> Goat
> Lion
> Monkey. *See* Animal musician–Ape
> Porcupine
> Rabbit
> Ram

Anjou, François, duc de. *See* Francois, duc d'Anjou
Anna (prophetess). *See* Christ–Presentation in the Temple
Anne, duc de Joyeuse
Anne, Duchess of Bedford
Anne of Brittany
Announcement, public, with music
Annunciation. *See* Virgin–Annunciation
Annunciation to the Shepherds. *See* Shepherds, Annunciation to
Antico, Andrea (publisher/printer)
Anthony of Dornstätt (fifer)
Antiphon. *See* Mass and Office–Antiphon
Antiphon, Marian. *See* Mass and Office–Antiphon, Marian
Antiphonal performance
Antiphonary. *See* Text, liturgical– Antiphonary
Aphrodite/Venus. *See also* Planets, music associated with– Venus
Apocalypse. *See* Apocalypse, Elders of; Text– Bible– Revelation; Text–Biblical
> adaptation; individual apocalypses by name, e.g., Apocalypse of Saint-Sever.
Apocalypse–Adoration of Lamb
Apocalypse, Elders of
Apocalypse of Saint-Sever
Apocalypse series (Dürer)
Apocalypse–Seven angels with trumpets
Apocalypse–Throne of God
Apollo
Apollo and Marsyas
Apollo and Muses
Apollo slays Python
Apostles. *See* Blessed; Virgin–Assumption; Virgin–Death
Aquarius. *See* Zodiacal signs–Aquarius
Aquinas, Thomas. *See* St. Thomas Aquinas
Aquinas, Thomas, triumph of. *See* Triumph of St. Thomas Aquinas
Arabel (in Willehalm)
Aragon, Ferrante I, King of. *See* Ferrante I, King of Aragon and Naples
Arbeau, Thoinot
Arcadelt, Jacques
Ares/Mars. *See also* Planets, music associated with–Mars
Argus, King
Ariadne
Arion

Aristotle
Arithmetic. *See* Liberal arts–Arithmetic
Arius
Ark, Return of. *See* David–Return of the Ark
Arluno, Bianca Pellegrini d'. *See* Pellegrini d'Arluno, Bianca
Armenbibel (Biblia pauperum). *See* Text–Biblical adaptation
Arms, coat of. *See* Escutcheon, musical
Arndes, Steffen (publisher/printer)
Arnive, Queen (of Arthurian legend)
Arnoldus Misnensis, Lectionary of. *See* Lectionary of Arnoldus Misnensis
Artemis Britomartis
Artemis/Diana, temple of
Arthur, King
Arthurian legend
Artist and music (a musical subject in an artist's studio)
Artus (lutenist)
Asaph
Aspis and music
Assumption of the Virgin. *See* Virgin–Assumption
Astrological treatise. *See* Text, didactic–Astronomy or astrology
Astronomical treatise. *See* Text, didactic–Astronomy or astrology
Astronomy. *See* Liberal arts–Astronomy
Athena/Minerva
Athena/Minerva, festival of
Athena/Minerva, temple of
Athletic event, music at
Atre Périlleux, L'
Atropos. *See* Fates–Atropos
Aubert, David
Augsburg
Augustin (cornettist)
Aupres de vous. *See* Chanson–Aupres de vous
Austria. *See* Trieberg; Weissenhorn
Austria, Leopold I of. *See* Leopold I of Austria
Austria, Mariana of, Queen of Spain. *See* Mariana of Austria, Queen of Spain
Ave regina coelorum. *See* Mass and Office–Antiphon, Marian–Ave regina
    coelorum
Averroes
Babylon
Bacchanal. *See* Ceremony, religious–Pagan
Bacchante
Bacchante musician
Bacchus/Dionysus
Bacchus/Dionysus, cult of
Bade, Josse (publisher/printer)
Balbulus, Notker. *See* Notker Balbulus
Baldini Calendar. *See* Calendar, Baldini
Ball. *See* Dancing, couple
Ballet. *See* Dancing, theatrical; Theater–Costume design–Ballet; Theater–Stage
    setting–Ballet
Ballet des Polonais, Le (Beaujoyeulx)
Balletto de cavallo. *See* Dancing–Horse ballet

Balthasar (Magus). *See* Christ–Adoration of the Magi; Magi

Banquet. *See* Meal, music at

Baprechtswile, Albrecht, Marchschal von. *See* Albrecht, Marchschal von Baprechtswile

Barcelona

Bargagli, Girolamo

Barnabas

Basel

Basel–Haus zum Tanz

Basse dance. *See* Dancing–Basse dance

Bath, music in

Bathsheba. *See* David and Bathsheba

Baton. *See* Conducting–Baton

Battle of Jericho. *See* Jericho, battle of

Battle of Marvelle. *See* Marvelle, battle of

Battle of Ravenna. *See* Ravenna, battle of

Bauer (jester)

Bavaria, Albrecht IV of. *See* Albrecht IV of Bavaria

Bavaria, Wilhelm V, Duke of. *See* Wilhelm V, Duke of Bavaria

Baza, conquest of

Beati qui audiunt verbum dei. *See* Motet–Beati qui audiunt verbum dei

Beatus de Liebana

Beatus manuscript. *See* Beatus de Liebana

Beatus page. *See* Text–Bible–Psalm 1

Beaujoyeulx, Baltasar de

Bed, Perilous (of Arthurian legend). *See* Gawain on Perilous Bed

Bedford, Anne, Duchess of. *See* Anne, Duchess of Bedford

Bedford, Duke of (John of Lancaster, Hours of. *See* Hours of the Duke of Bedford

Bedford Hours. *See* Hours of the Duke of Bedford

Beggar. *See* Street musician

Bell-making. *See* Instrument-making–Bell

Belles Heures de Jean duc de Berry. *See* Hours–Belles Heures de Jean duc de Berry

Belvoir Psalter. *See* Psalter, Belvoir

Bénoît de Sainte-More: Roman de Troie

Berg, Adam (publisher/printer)

Berg, Johannes

Bergmann von Olpe (publisher/printer)

Berkshire, England

Bermudo, Juan

Bernard von Cles. *See* Clesius, Cardinal Bernhardus

Bernhard von Breydenbach

Berry, Belles Heures de Jean duc de. *See* Hours–Belles Heures de Jean duc de Berry

Berry, Jean duc de. *See* Jean duc de Berry

Berry, Très-Belles Heures de Jean duc de. *See* Hours–Très-Belles Heures de Jean duc
   de Berry

Berwald, Jacob, heirs of (publisher/printer)

Bestiary. *See* Text, didactic; Natural history–Bestiary

Beyer, Johannes (publisher/printer)

Bezieres, Ermengaud de. *See* Ermengaud de Bezieres

Bibiena, Ferdinando Galli

Bible. *See* Text–Bible; Text–Biblical adaptation; individual Bibles by name, e.g.,
   Bible, Carilef

Bible, Carilef

Bible historiale. *See* Text–Biblical adaptation
Bible, Lübeck
Bible of Borso d'Este
Bible of Charles the Bald, First. *See* Bible, Vivian
Bible, Velislav's
Bible, Vivian
Biblia pauperum. *See* Text–Biblical adaptation
Billingsley, H.
Binchois, Gilles
Biography. *See* Text, historical–Biography
Bird song
Birth, symbol of
Blessed (groups of saints, martyrs, virgins, patriarchs, prophets, confessors, apostles,
    etc. found in scenes depicting heaven by whatever name [the City of God, the
    New Jerusalem, etc.]). *See also* David and Blessed; Last Judgment
Blessed and Damned. *See* Last Judgment
Bligge von Steinach, Her
Boccaccio, Giovanni
Boccaccio—Ameto
Boccaccio—Decameron
Boehmen. *See* Bohemia
Boethian categories of music. *See* Musica mundana, humana, instrumentalis
Boethius
Bohemia. *See* Passional of Kunigunde von Böhmen; Prague
Bohemia, Wenzel II, King of. *See* Wenzel II, King of Bohemia
Boleyn, Anne
Bolognini, Matteo Attendolo. *See* Matteo Attendolo Bolognini
Bonanni, Filippo
Book of hours. *See* Text–Hours; individual books of hours by name, e.g., "Hours
    of Jeanne d'Evreux"
Book of Martyrs. *See* Martyrs, Book of
Borso d'Este. *See* Este, Borso d'
Boston Throne. *See* Throne, Boston
Botho, Conrad
Bourgeois music. *See* Informal music-making
Brabant, François, duc d'Anjou, Duke of. *See* François, duc d'Anjou
Braccifori family
Brandenburg, Otto von. *See* Otto von Brandenburg, Markgraf
Brangaene (of Arthurian legend)
Brant, Sebastian
Brant, Sebastian–Ship of Fools
Braun, Georg
Breslau, Heinrich von. *See* Heinrich von Pressela, Herzoge
Breuil, Juan de–Le Jouvencel
Breviary. *See* Text, liturgical–Breviary; individual breviaries by name, e.g., Breviary
    of Philippe le Bon
Breviary of Love. *See* Ermengaud de Bezieres–Breviary of Love
Breviary of Philippe le Bon
Breviary of René II
Breviary, Salisbury
Breydenbach, Bernhard von. *See* Bernhard von Breydenbach
Brittany, Anne of. *See* Anne of Brittany

Bromholm Psalter. *See* Psalter, Bromholm
Bronescomb, Walter, Bishop of Exeter
Brothel, music in. *See* Harlot musician
Bruck, Arnold von
Bruno von Hornberg
Brussels Hours. *See* Hours, Brussels
Bruyn, Abraham
Buccinate. *See* Musical term–*Buccinate*
Buechein, von
Bueil, Juan de. *See* Breuil, Juan de
Buonanni, Filippo. *See* Bonanni, Filippo
Burgundy, Duke of (which one not known)
Burgundy, Mary of. *See* Mary of Burgundy
Burgundy, Philippe le Bon, Duke of. *See* Philippe le Bon
Buti, Francesco
Cadiz
Caesar, Julius
Caesar, Julius, triumph of. *See* Triumph of Caesar
Calderini, Andrea
Calendar. *See* Months, music associated with; Seasons, music associated with; Text,
    didactic–Calendar
Calendar, Baldini
Calliope. *See* Muses–Calliope
Cambridge Psalter. *See* Psalter, Cambridge
Cámera, Juan Rodrígues de la. *See* Juan Rodrígues de la Cámera
Cana. *See* Christ–Miracles–Cana
Canon
Canon–Prenez sur moi vostre exemple
Canon–Vincenti dabo nomen novum
Canonical hours. *See* Ceremony, religious–Judaeo-Christian (depiction of service)
Cantata–Celebrate col canto di Luigi immortalla gloria
Cantate. *See* Musical term–*Cantate*
Canterbury Psalter. *See* Psalter, Canterbury
Canterey. *See* Musical term–*Canterey* [lit]
Canticis. *See* Musical term–*Canticis* [lit]
Canticle of Hezekiah (Isaiah 38:10-20)
Canticle of Moses
Cantico. *See* Musical term–*Cantico* [lit]
Canticum. *See* Musical term–*Canticum*
Canticum. *See* Musical term–*Canticum* [lit]
Cantigas de Santa Maria
Cantike. *See* Musical term–*Cantike* [lit]
Cantionum. *See* Musical term–*Cantionum* [lit]
Cantorey. *See* Musical term–*Cantorey* [lit]
Canzona
Capistrum. *See* Cheek-band
Caprioli, Carlo
Car or float, musician on
Cards, playing–Tarocchi
Carilef Bible. *See* Bible, Carilef
Carmen
Carmen. *See* Musical term–*Carmen* [lit]

Chartres, Duke and Duchess of
Chastity personified. *See also* Virtues and vices personified; Virtues–Chastity
Cheek-band (capistrum)
Chess game, music at. *See* Game, music at–Chess
Chevalier, Etienne
Chevalier, Etienne, Hours of. *See* Hours of Etienne Chevalier
Chevrot, Jean, Bishop of Tournai
Chichester Cathedral
Chigi family
Chiron
Choirbook. *See also* Music book; Music sheet
Choris. *See* Musical term–*Choris* [lit]
Choro. *See* Musical term–*Choro* [lit]
Chorus. *See* Musical term–*Chorus* [lit]
Chrétien de Troyes–Conte del Graal
Christ. *See also* Last Judgment; Trinity; various subentries under Virgin
Christ–Adoration of the Magi
Christ–Adoration of the Shepherds
Christ–Among the Doctors
Christ and Evangelist symbols. *See also* Apocalypse–Throne of God
Christ–Ascension
Christ–Baptism
Christ–Bearing Cross
Christ–Before Pilate
Christ–Betrayal
Christ, birth of. *See* Christ–Nativity
Christ–Blessing. *See* Christ
Christ Child. *See* Christ musician; Christ–Nativity; St. Christopher; Virgin and Child; Virgin and Child–In garden
Christ–Crucifixion
Christ–Enthroned. *See* Christ; Christ and Evangelist symbols; Apocalypse–Throne of God
Christ–Entombment
Christ–Flagellation
Christ–Flight into Egypt
Christ–Harrowing of hell
Christ–Holy Women at Sepulchre
Christ in mandorla. *See* Christ
Christ–Lamb of God
Christ–Miracles
Christ–Miracles–Cana
Christ–Miracles–Raising Lazarus
Christ–Mocking
Christ musician
Christ–Nativity. *See also* Christ–Adoration of the Magi; Christ–Adoration of the Shepherds
Christ–Parables–Lazarus and Rich Man
Christ–Preaching
Christ–Presentation in the Temple
Christ–Resurrection
Christ–Showing wounds
Christ–Temptation

Christine of Lorraine

Christus natus est nobis. *See* Mass and Office–Invitatory–Christus natus est nobis

Chronicle. *See* Text, historical–Chronicle

Chronicle, Cologne. *See* Cologne Chronicle

Chronicle, Nuremberg. *See* Nuremberg Chronicle

Chronicle of France

Chronicle of Matthew Paris

Chronicle, Saxon. *See* Saxon Chronicle

Chronicles, Books of. *See* Text–Bible–Chronicles

Church mode. *See* Mode, church

Church, music directly outside

Church, music inside

Church, Triumph of. *See* Triumph of Church

Ciconia, Johannes

Cinq Sens, Les (series)

City of God. *See* Angel musician; Angel musician, wingless; Blessed

Civic music

Cleric playing instrument (including those holding bells)

Cleric singing. *See also* Singing, sacred; Singing, secular

Clesius, Cardinal Bernhardus (Bernard von Cles)

Clio. *See* Muses–Clio

Clotho. *See* Fates–Clotho

Clovis I, King

Cluny Capitals

Coat of arms. *See* Escutcheon, musical

Coclico, Adriaen Petit

Coclicus, Adriaen. *See* Coclico

Cocq, Captain Frans Banning

Cologne

Cologne Chronicle

Colonna, Antonio

Comestor, Petrus. *See also* Text–Biblical adaptation (Bible historiale)

Commedia dell'arte. *See* Theatrical spectacle with music–Commedia dell'arte; Theater–Costume design–Commedia dell'arte; Theater–Stage setting–Commedia dell'arte

Complete instrumentarium. *See* Instrumentarium, complete

Concordantz. *See* Musical term–*Concordantz* [lit]

Conducting

Conducting–Baton

Conrad von der Rosen

Conrad von Rot

Constantinople

Conte del Graal. *See* Chrétien de Troyes–Conte del Graal

Contest, musical

Conty, Princess de

Corbetta, Francesco

Corneyt. *See* Musical Term–*Corneyt*

Cornwall, Richard Earl of. *See* Richard, Earl of Cornwall

Coronation

Coronation of the Virgin. *See* Virgin–Coronation

Corvinus, Matthias. *See* Matthias Corvinus, King of Hungary

Cosimo I de' Medici. *See* Medici, Cosimo I de'

Costume. *See* Theater–Costume design; Text, didactic–Costumes
Cotin, Nicolas
Count Vivian's Bible. *See* Bible, Vivian
Country fair. *See* Rustic music
Court, music at (music performed by or for rulers or their courtiers; the picture need not show a court). *See also* David and Saul; Herod, feast of
Court, music at–Minnesinger
Court musician. *See* Court, music at
Courtroom. *See* Law court
Creation. *See also* Adam and Eve
Credo Tapestry. *See* Tapestry, Credo
Creed, Apostles
Cremona
Crescentius, Petrus
Cries, street. *See* Street cry
Crossing of the Red Sea. *See* Red Sea, crossing of
Cumae, Sibyl of. *See* Sibyl of Cumae
Cupid. *See* Eros/Cupid
Cwidum. *See* Musical term–*Cwidum* [lit]
Cybele, cult of
Cyclops
Dame à la licorne, La, Tapestries. *See* Tapestries, La dame à la licorne
Damned and Blessed. *See* Last Judgment
Damon. *See* Thyrsis and Damon
Dampierre, Guy de, Count of Flanders, Psalter of. *See* Psalter of Guy de Dampierre
Dance instruction. *See* Instruction, dance; Text, didactic– Dance
Dance instruction book. *See* Text, didactic– Dance
Dance of Death. *See also* Memento mori
Dance of Death (series)
Dancing
Dancing, ballet. *See* Dancing, theatrical; Theater–Costume design–Ballet; Theater–Stage setting–Ballet
Dancing--Basse dance
Dancing–Branle
Dancing–Carol. *See* Dancing, round
Dancing–Choro. *See also* Musical term–*Choro* [lit]
Dancing, couple
Dancing–Horse ballet
Dancing–Ländler--Wickeln
Dancing–Moresque
Dancing, religious
Dancing, round (includes carol)
Dancing, solo
Dancing–Les sonnettes
Dancing–Sword dance
Dancing, theatrical (includes ballet)
Dancing, theatrical–Wild men
Dancing–Volte
Daniel's Copy Book
Dante Alighieri
Dante Alighieri–Divina Commedia
Dardenay, Jean

Darmstadt. *See* Anthony of Dornstätt
Daughter of Jephthah. *See* Jephthah and daughter
David
David alone
David among heroes
David and Bathsheba
David and Blessed
David and Goliath
David and musicians (David with Asaph, Ethan, Heman and Jeduthrun, or David with
    one or more miscellaneous musicians; *not* Jesse Tree or David–Return of the Ark,
    etc.)
David and Samuel
David and Saul
David anointed king. *See* David and Samuel
David as psalmist. *See also* David alone; David and musicians
David as shepherd
David greeted by the Israelites. *See* David, triumph of
David in Jesse Tree. *See* Jesse Tree
David–Return of the Ark
David, triumph of (1 Sam. 18:6)
Day, John (publisher/printer)
Death. *See* Dance of death; Funeral, music at; Memento mori
Death, dance of. *See* Dance of Death
Death personified. *See* Dance of Death; Memento mori
Death, symbol of. *See* Memento mori
Decameron. *See* Boccaccio–Decameron
Decretals. *See* Text, legal–Decretals
Dee, John
Demetrios
Demon. *See* Devil; Devil musician
Desperando spero. *See* Motet–Desperando spero
Devereux, Robert, Earl of Essex
Devil. *See also* Christ–Temptation; Devil musician; St. Anthony–Temptation
Devil musician
Dialectic. *See* Liberal arts–Dialectic
Diana. *See* Artemis/Diana
Diaz, Francisco (publisher/printer)
Didactic text. *See* Text, didactic
Diepolt von Slandersberg
Dinadan
Dinteville, Jean de
Diocletian, Emperor
Dionysus. *See* Bacchus/Dionysus
Ditié. *See* Musical term–*Ditié* [lit]
Diurnal. *See* Text, liturgical–Diurnal
Dives. *See* Christ–Parables–Lazarus and Rich Man
Divina Commedia. *See* Dante Alighieri–Divina Commedia
Divinity, Triumph of. *See* Triumph of Divinity
Domestic music. *See* Informal music-making
Domine fiant anima. *See* Motet–Domine fiant anima
Donato, Bishop Pietro
Donne, Sir John

Donne Triptych. *See* Altar–Donne Triptych
Dorat, Jean
Dornstätt, Anthony of. *See* Anthony of Dornstätt
Douairière de Billebahaut, La. See Theater–Costume design–Ballet–*Douairière de Billebahaut*; Theater–Stage setting–Ballet–*Douairière de Billebahaut*
Dove of the Holy Spirit. *See* Holy Spirit, Dove of; Trinity
Drama. *See* Text, literary– Drama; Theater; Theatrical spectacle with music; names of individual dramas
Drama with music. *See* Theatrical spectacle with music
Drayton, Michael
Dudley, Robert, Earl of Leicester
Duet
Dufay, Guillaume
Dunstable, John
Duo. *See* Duet
Du Pré, Denis (publisher/printer)
Dürer, Albrecht (author)
Dürer, Albrecht (portrait)
Dwarf musician
Dyweynndle (jester)
Eadwine Psalter. *See* Psalter, Eadwine
Ebersheim
Echo
Eclogues. *See* Virgil–Eclogues
Edom
Egypt, Flight into. *See* Christ–Flight into Egypt
Egypt, King of
Egypt, Queen of
Ehebrecherbrücke des Königs Artus (series)
Eicheister family
Elder of the Apocalypse. *See* Apocalypse, Elder of
Elements, four–Earth
Elizabeth I
Elizabeth of Lotharingia
Elizabeth, Queen of Hungary
Eman. *See* Heman
Emperor. *See* names of individual emperors
Ems, Rudolph von. *See* Rudolph von Ems
Encomium musices (series)
Enfant prodique, L'
England. *See* Berkshire; Chichester; Wadley
England, Elizabeth I of. *See* Elizabeth I
Envy personified
Ephraim
Epic. *See* Text, literary–Romance or epic; names of individual texts
Epiphany. *See* Christ–Adoration of the Magi
Epiphany (Twelfth Night) celebration, music at
Erato. *See* Muses–Erato
Ermengaud de Bezieres–Breviary of Love
Eros/Cupid
Eschenbach, Wolfram von. *See* Wolfram von Eschenbach
Escutcheon, musical

Flight into Egypt. *See* Christ–Flight into Egypt

Florence, Neroni family of. *See* Neroni family of Florence

Florence, Pandolfini family of. *See* Pandolfini family of Florence

Florence–Piazza S. Croce

Florence–Piazza S. Giovanni

Florence–Uffizi

Fluster. See Musical term–*Fluster* [lit]

Folly personified. *See also* Ship of Fools

Fool or jester. *See also* Ship of Fools

Fool or jester musician

Footrest

Forest, Comte de. *See* Liziart, comte de Forest

Formschneider, Hieronymus (publisher/printer)

Foxe, John

France. *See* Paris; Rheims; Versailles. *See also* Medici, Catherine de', Queen of France; Charles V of France; Charles IX of France; Chronicle of France; Francis I, King of France; Henry III, King of France, Louis

Francis I, King of France

François, duc d'Anjou, Count of Flanders, Duke of Brabant

Fratrum Servorum S. Mariae, Missale. *See* Missale Fratrum Servorum S. Mariae

Frauenlob (Wrouewenlob), Meister Heinrich Meissen

Freydal

Fridolin, Stefan

Frye, Walter

Fugger family

Funeral, music at

Gabriel, Archangel. *See* Virgin–Annunciation

Gafurius, Franchinus

Galahad

Gallery, musicians'

Gallus, Jacobus. *See* Handl, Jacob

Game, music at

Game, music at–Chess

Ganassi, Silvestro di

Gandin (of Arthurian legend)

Garden music (music performed in a cultivated outdoor space often, but not necessarily, enclosed). *See also* Virgin and Child–In garden; Informal music-making outdoors

Garden of love. *See* Musical couple

Gaudeamus omnes. *See* Mass and Office–Introit–Gaudeamus omnes

Gawain on Perilous Bed

Gayart des Moulins. *See* Guyart des Moulins

Genesis, Book of. *See* Text–Bible–Genesis

Genius (Genii). *See* Angel musician; Angel musician, wingless; Poet as Creator; Putto musician; Putto musician, winged

Geometry. *See* Liberal arts–Geometry

Georg of Murbach, Abbot

Gerlach, Dietrich (publisher/printer)

Germany. *See* Augsburg; Cologne; Hamburg; Munich; Nuremberg; Passau; Stade; Steinen; Wittemberg

Getar, Her

Ghent Altar. *See* Altar, Ghent

Gylyme (fool)
Haarlem
Hadlob, Meister Johans
Haggadah. *See* Text–Haggadah
Hamburg
Handl, Jacob
Harlot musician
Harvesting. *See* Rustic music
Hassler, Hans Leo
Hearing, allegory of. *See* Senses, allegory of–Hearing
Heaven. *See* Angel musician; Angel musician, wingless; Blessed; Putto musician; Putto
    musician, winged
Hebrew music. *See* Jewish music
Heinrich, Landgraf von Hessen
Heinrich von Ofterdingen
Heinrich von Pressela (Breslau), Herzoge
Heinrich von Stretlingen, Der
Helicon, Mount. *See* Mount Helicon
Helios. *See* Sun personified
Hell
Heman
Henry III, King of France
Hera/Juno
Herald. *See* Announcement, public, with music
Hercules. *See also Histori Herculis*
Hercules musician
Hermann von Thüringen
Hermes/Mercury. *See also* Planets, music associated with–Mercury
Herod
Herod, feast of
Herod–Massacre of the Innocents. *See* Massacre of Innocents
Herodias. *See* Herod, feast of
Heroes, Nine
Heroes, Nine–Hebrew heroes
Heroes, Nine–Pagan heroes
Heroes, Nine, Tapestries. *See* Tapestries, Nine Heroes
Herrad von Landsberg
Hessen, Heinrich, Landgraf von. *See* Heinrich, Landgraf von Hessen
Hezekiah
Hexit
Hezekiah, Canticle of. *See* Canticle of Hezekiah
Higman, Nicolas (publisher/printer)
Hiltboldt von Swanegoer, Her
Hippocrene (spring sacred to poets)
Histori Herculis
Historical text. *See* Text, historical
History of Abraham Tapestries. *See* Tapestries, History of Abraham
Hochzeitstänzer (series)
Hofhaimer, Paul
Holland. *See* Haarlem; Utrecht
Holy Ghost. *See* Holy Spirit, Dove of; Trinity
Holy Spirit, Dove of

Homer

Honor personified

Horace

Hornberg, Bruno von. *See* Bruno von Hornberg

Horse ballet. *See* Dancing—Horse ballet

Horse race. *See* Athletic event, music at

Hours—Belles Heures de Jean duc de Berry

Hours, book of. *See* Text—Hours; books of hours listed by name, e.g., Hours—Belles Heures de Jean duc de Berry; Hours of Jeanne d'Evreux

Hours, Brussels

Hours, canonical. *See* Ceremony, religious—Judaeo-Christian (depiction of service); Text—Hours

Hours of Etienne Chevalier

Hours of Jeanne de'Evreux

Hours of Louis de Laval

Hours of the Duke of Bedford

Hours, Pembroke Book of

Hours—Très-Belles Heures de Jean duc de Berry

House music. *See* Informal music-making indoors

Housebook, Medieval

Hrabanus Maurus

Hugh of St. Victor

Humanist musician (a single musician playing lute or lira da braccio or singing to a group in a room [often a classroom] or gathered around him in a city street; when indoors there is often a podium at which he stands or sits)

Humors, four

Hungary, Elizabeth, Queen of. *See* Elizabeth, Queen of Hungary

Hungary, Mathias Corvinus, King of. *See* Mathias Corvinus, King of Hungary

Hunterian Psalter. *See* Psalter, Hunterian

Hunting

Hygieia

Hymn—Jesu redemptor omnium

Hymn—Verbum caro factum est

Idithun. *See* Jeduthun

Ignorance personified

Image of world. *See* World image

Incoronazione di Poppea, L'. See Opera—*Incoronazione di Poppea* (Monteverdi)

Informal music-making (music, solo or ensemble, performed by middle- or upper-class urban dwellers, not in a courtly setting [as opposed to academy, church, court, military, rustic, or tavern music])

Informal music-making indoors

Informal music-making outdoors. *See also* Garden music

Inspiration. *See* Poet as Creator

Instruction book, musical. *See* Text, didactic—Music. *See also* Instruction, musical

Instruction, dance

Instruction, musical. *See also* Text, didactic—Music

Instrument and singing. *See* Singing sacred—With instruments; Singing, secular—With instruments

Instrument case

Instrument case—Aulos/tibia

Instrument case—Flute/recorder

Instrument case—Guitar

Instrument case–Harp
Instrument case–Lute
Instrument case–Recorder. *See also* Instrument case–Flute/recorder
Instrument case–Shawm
Instrument case–Trombone
Instrument-making
Instrument-making–Bell
Instrument-making–Harpsichord
Instrument-making–Lute
Instrument, pseudo- (ancient and non-Western instruments in Western medieval,
    Renaissance, and Baroque sources; unreal instruments invented by an artist,
    intentionally or unintentionally, after a classical or other source; parodies of
    real instruments, such as bowed rakes, plucked jawbones, etc.)
Instrument reference to. (An instrument is listed when the name is visible on the
    page or when the author of the bibliographical source says it is there. In order
    to preserve the original as closely as possible, keep the grammatical case in which
    the instrument is mentioned. An instrument reference followed by "[lit]" indi-
    cates there is no picture of the instrument, but it is mentioned in the text. Check
    the entire list for variations of the instrument name; the great number of vari-
    ations in terminology and spelling do not permit cross-referencing.) *See also* sub-
    entries under Musical term (e.g., Musical term–*Vedelede*); subentries under
    Musician, reference to (e.g., Musician, reference to–*Fiedler*).
Instrument, reference to–*Ampos und hemmer*
                    Avena
                    Bimaen
                    Bombardt
                    Britschen
                    Buccina
                    Buccinae
                    Buccine
                    Buisine
                    Buisuine
                    Busaŭn
                    Bymaen
                    Byman
                    Chordis
                    Chorus
                    Cimbalum
                    Cithara
                    Cithara [lit]
                    Citharam
                    Citharas
                    Clareta
                    Clavicimbalum
                    Claviciterium
                    Clavicordium
                    Cordis
                    Cornu
                    Cymbalis
                    Cymbalum
                    Cytera Jheronimi
                    Cythara

Instrument, reference to—*Cythara* [lit]
  Cythara Jheronimi
  Decachordo
  Decacordo
  Diseincordei
  Eaerpungum
  Estrumenz
  Felttrümet
  Fistula
  Fistula Hieronimi
  Flōten
  Fydel
  Geig
  Geige
  Geigen, Clein
  Geigen, Gross
  Gemsenhorn
  Glocke
  Glocken
  Hackbrett
  Hafen
  Hakpret
  Harpe
  Harpe [lit]
  Harpes
  Harpfen
  Harpff
  Heaerpaen
  Hearpan
  Hearperas [lit]
  Heortan
  Herpaucken
  Herpe
  Horn, Acher
  Horn, Byme
  Horn, Thurner
  Hylsongae
  Instrumenz de menustracye
  Jägerhorn
  Jeger horn
  Jegerhoren, Krump Niderlendisch
  Jegerhoren, Teutsche
  Krumhörner
  Krumhorn
  Krump Niderlendisch Jegerhoren
  Krump selzam horen
  Krumpen hörner, Niderlendischen
  Krumphörner
  Kuschellen
  Laut
  Laute
  Lauten

Instrument, reference to—*Lauten, Grosse*
Lautten
Leyer
Lira
Luten
Lyra
Musica
Orgaenum
Organa
Organan
Organistrum
Organo
Organum
Organum Hieronimi
Orgel
Orgne
Paücklin, Clein
Pfeiff
Pfeiffen
Pfiffen [lit]
Platerspil
Portative
Posaun
Posaunen
Positiff
Positive
Possetif
Psaeltere
Psalterii
Psalterio
Psalterio decachordo
Psalterio decacordo
Psalterio decem cordarum
Psalterio decemchordarum
Psalterio deci cordarum
Psalterium
Psalterium [lit]
Psalterium decacordum
Psaltero
Psalterum tyen strenga
Pumphart
Pusaunen
Quintern
Rauschpfeiffen
Rauschpfeiffen, Grosse
Rauschpfeiffen, Klain
Regal
Regale
Ribeben
Rigal
Russpfeif
Russpfeiff [lit]

Instrument, reference to—*Rybeben*
Rygal
Sackpfeiff
Sackpfeiff [lit]
Sackpfiff
Sackpfiff [lit]
Sackpfiffen
Saelterae
Saeltere
Saelterio
Salter
Saltere [lit]
Salterii
Saltier
Saltier [lit]
Saltier de dis cordes
Saltier diseincorde
Saltre tien strengan
Schalmey
Schalmeyen
Schalmeyen possetif
Scheidtholtt
Schelle
Schellen
Scholmayen
Schwegel
Seittenspyel [lit]
Sistris
Spaltere
Swegas
Swege
Swieg
Tämerlin
Tammerlin
Timpanan
Timpane
Timpano
Timpanum
Tin strengum
Trommet
Trumpeln
Trumscheidt
Trumscheit
Tuba
Tuba [lit]
Tuba Hieronimi
Tubae
Tubae corneae
Tube
Tube cornee
Tube cornee [lit]
Tubis

Instrument, reference to–*Tubis ductilibus*
                                 Tubis ductilibus [lit]
                                 Tympane
                                 Tympanis
                                 Tympano
                                 Tympanum
                                 Tympanum [lit]
                                 Tympanum Jheronimi
                                 Tymphanum
                                 Virginal
                                 Vyole
                                 Waldthoren
                                 Waldthoren, Gross
                                 Zincken
                                 Zinckhen
                                 Zinkenhorn
                                 Zwerchpfeiff
                                 Zymbalum Jheronimi
                                 Zymeln
                                 Zynngken
Instrument support–Stick
Instrument support–Strap
Instrumentalist, reference to. *See* Musician, reference to
Instrumentarium, complete (a more or less systematic survey of all musical instruments or at least of all categories of instruments). *See also* Angel musician
Interlude. *See* Intermedio
Intermedio
Intermedio–*Pellegrina, La* (Girolamo Bargagli)
Intermezzo. *See* Intermedio
Introit. *See* Mass and Office–Introit
Investiture, knightly
Invitatory. *See* Mass and Office–Invitatory
Io
Iphitos
Isabella Clara Eugenia, Archduchess
Isabella d'Este. *See* Este, Isabella d'
Isaiah
Isaiah, Book of. *See* Text–Bible–Isaiah
Isenheim Altar. *See* Altar, Isenheim
Isis, cult of
Isolde. *See also* Tristan
Isolde of Brittany
Israelites. *See* David, Triumph of
Italy. *See* Ceneda; Florence; Gubbio; Lucca; Naples; Padua; Parma; Ravenna; Rome; Siena; Urbino
Itonje (of Arthurian legend)
Itzehoe
Jacotin (composer)
Janus
Jason
J'ay pris amours. *See* Chanson–J'ay pris amours
Jean duc de Berry

Liberal arts—Rhetoric
Liebana, Beatus de. *See* Beatus de Liebana
Liechtenstein, Petrus (publisher/printer)
Lied—"Mein fleiss und müh" (Senfl)
Lieder. *See* Musical term—*Lieder* [lit]
Linos
Litany. *See* Ceremony, religious—Judaeo-Christian (depiction of service)
Literary text. *See* Text, literary; names of individual texts
Liziart, comte de Forest
Logrono, Diego Ximenes de Enciso Vezino of. *See* Vezino, Diego Ximenes de Enciso, of Logrono
Lomatio, Johannes Petrus de (publisher/printer)
Lombards, Theodolinda, Queen of. *See* Theodolinda, Queen of the Lombards
London—Stahlhof
Lord's Prayer (Matthew 6:9-13). *See* Oraison dominicale
Lorenzo di Pierfrancesco Medici. *See* Medici, Lorenzo de Pierfrancesco
Lorraine, Christine of. *See* Christine of Lorraine
Lorraine, Margarethe of. *See* Margarethe of Lorraine
Lothair, Emperor
Lothair Psalter. *See* Psalter, Lothair
Lotharingia, Elizabeth of. *See* Elizabeth of Lotharingia
Lotharingia, René II of. *See* René II of Lotharingia
Lotti, L.
Louis IX of France. *See also* Text—Hours—Office of St. Louis
Louis XII
Louis XIII
Louis XIV
Louis, Guillaume de
Louterell Psalter. *See* Psalter, Luttrell
Louterell, Sir Geoffrey. *See* Luttrell, Sir Geoffrey
Love, Castle of, siege of. *See* Castle of Love, siege of
Love, Garden of. *See* Musical couple
Love, Triumph of. *See* Triumph of Love
Lucan (Marcus Annaeus Lucanus)
Lucca
Lucène, Fernando de. *See* Fernando de Lucène
Ludovisi Throne. *See* Throne, Ludovisi
Lübeck Bible. *See* Bible, Lübeck
Lübeck, Vincent
Luke, Book of. *See* Text—Bible—Luke
Lully, Jean Baptiste
Luther, Martin
Luttrell Psalter. *See* Psalter, Luttrell
Luttrell, Sir Geoffrey
Luxuria personified. *See* Virtues and vices personified—Vices—Luxuria
Lyric poetry. *See* Text, literary—Lyric poetry; individual titles by name
Lystra (Asia Minor)
Machiavelli, Niccolò
Madonna. *See* Virgin
Madrid
Madrigal
Maenad. *See* Bacchante

Magi

Magi, Adoration of. *See* Christ–Adoration of the Magi

Mahaut (shepherd)

Maine, Duchess du

Maitland, John, Duke of Lauderdale

Malvagna Triptych. *See* Altar–Malvagna Triptych

Manasseh

Manessische Lieder MS

Mankind personified

Marenzio, Luca

Margarethe of Lorraine

Margherita Theresa, Infanta of Spain

Marginal ornament, musical

Maria Theresa, Infanta of Spain

Mariage à la campagne, Le

Marian Antiphon. *See* Mass and Office–Antiphon, Marian

Mariana of Austria, Queen of Spain

Mark, King (of Arthurian legend)

Mars. *See* Ares/Mars; Planets, music associated with–Mars

Marsyas. *See also* Apollo and Marsyas

Martyrdom. *See* Execution, music at

Martyrs, Book of

Marvelle, battle of

Mary. *See* Virgin

Mary Magdalene. *See* St. Mary Magdalene

Mary of Burgundy

Masquerade (costumed figures, no masks necessary). *See also* Theater; Theatrical spectacle with music

Mass. *See* Ceremony, religious–Judaeo-Christian (for pictures of the religious service); Mass and Office (for pictures of music books or sheets with visible musical notation of the Mass or Office)

Mass and Office. *See also* Hymn

Mass and Office–Antiphon, Marian–Alma redemptoris mater

Antiphon, Marian–Ave regina coelorum (anon. *a* 2)

Antiphon, Marian–Ave regina coelorum (W. Frye)

Antiphon, Marian–Regina coeli laetare

Gloria

Introit–Gaudeamus omnes

Invitatory–Christus natus est nobis

Kyrie

Massacre of the Innocents

Mathematics personified. *See also* Liberal arts

Matteo Attendolo Bolognini

Matthew, Book of. *See* Text–Bible–Matthew

Matthias Corvinus, King of Hungary

Maurus, Hrabanus. *See* Hrabanus Maurus

Maximilian I, Emperor

Meal, music at. *See also* Symposium

Medici, Catherine de', Queen of France

Medici, Cosimo I de'

Medici, Ferdinand de'

Medici, Lorenzo di Pierfrancesco

Medicine and music

Medieval Housebook. *See* Housebook, Medieval

Mein fleiss und müh. *See* Lied—Mein fleiss und müh

Meissen, Heinrich von. *See* Frauenlob, Meister Heinrich

Meistersinger

Melancholy personified

Melchior (Magus). *See* Christ—Adoration of the Magi; Magi

Meliboeus

Melopoiae

Melpomene. *See* Muses—Melpomene

Memento mori (includes scenes in which instruments or musical activity are associated with the idea of death or with the transitory nature of worldly things, excepting scenes showing the dance of death or music at funerals). *See also* Dance of Death; Funeral, music at

Mendoza, Cardinal Pedro Gonzalez de

Menelaus

Mercury. *See* Hermes/Mercury; Planets, music associated with—Mercury

Mersenne, Marin

Metamorphoses. *See* Ovid—Metamorphoses

Meterschy (jester)

Methusala

Meung, Jean de

Midas

Middle-class music. *See* Informal music-making

Miélot, Jean

Milán, Luís

Military subjects (armies marching, battle scenes, military fanfares, music played by soldiers, etc.). *See also* Castle of Love, siege of; Ship, music in

Minerva. *See* Athena/Minerva

Minnesinger. *See* Court, music at—Minnesinger

Minstrel (a professional instrumentalist who belonged to a guild; minstrels functioned as court musicians, town musicians, and sometimes as street musicians and also accompanied church choirs). *See also* Civic music; Court, music at; Singing, sacred--With instruments; Street musician. For minstrels before 1400, *See* Jongleur. Trumpeters are listed as minstrels unless they fit into the categories "Military subjects" or "Announcement, public, with music"

Miriam

Miriam, Song of. *See* Red Sea, crossing of—Song of Miriam

Missal. *See* Text, liturgical—Missal; names of individual missals, e.g., Missale Fratrum Servorum S. Mariae

Missale Fratrum Servorum S. Mariae

Misnensis, Arnoldus, Lectionary of. *See* Lectionary of Arnoldus Misnensis

Moab

Mocking of Christ. *See* Christ—Mocking

Mode, church

Mode, church, personified

Moderne, Jacques (publisher/printer)

Molière (Jean Baptiste Poquelin)

Mon seul plaisir. *See* Chanson—Mon seul plaisir

Monster musician. *See* Grotesque musician

Montanar, Count and Countess of (in Willehalm)

Montanar, Island of (in Willehalm)

Montanus, Johannes. *See* Berg, Johannes

Montefeltro, Federigo da
Monterchio, Johannes de (scribe)
Monteverdi, Claudis
Months, music associated with–January
        May
        July
        October
        December
Months personified
Morellus, Fed. (publisher/printer)
Moresca. *See* Dancing–Moresque
Moresque. *See* Dancing–Moresque
Morgan Leaf
Morisque. *See* Dancing–Moresque
Morris dance. *See* Dancing–Moresque
Moses
Moses, Canticle of. *See* Canticle of Moses
Motet–Beati qui audiunt verbum dei (Luke 11:28)
Motet–Desperando spero
Motet–Domine fiant anima (Cornelius Schuyt *a 6*)
Moulins, Guyart des. *See* Guyart des Moulins
Mount Helicon
Mouton, Charles
Muiredach's Cross
Mummer. *See* Masquerade
Munich
Murbach, Georg of. *See* Georg of Murbach, Abbot
Muret, Antoine de
Muses. *See also* Apollo and the Muses
Muses–Calliope
   Clio
   Erato
   Euterpe
   Melpomene
   Polymnia
   Terpsichore
   Thalia
   Urania
Music as a Liberal art. *See* Liberal arts–Music
Music as a worldly pleasure (scenes which illustrate the concept of worldly, sinful, or illicit pleasures by means of musical subjects; implied is some contrast with spiritual pleasures or condemnation of secular music-making)
Music book (includes part books). *See also* Choirbook; Music sheet
Music, domestic. *See* Informal music-making
Music in taverns. *See* Tavern music
Music, military. *See* Military subjects
Music personified. *See also* Liberal arts–Music; Mode, church, personified; Winds, four, personified
Music personified with stag
Music roll. *See* Music sheet
Music, rustic. *See* Rustic music
Music school. *See* Instruction, musical

Music sheet (includes music rolls). *See also* Choirbook; Music book

Music stand. *See also* Choirbook (which always rests on a music stand)

Music stand–Person holding music

Music stand–Putto holding music

Music treatise. *See* Text, didactic–Music

Musica humana. *See* Musica mundana, humana, instrumentalis

Musica instrumentalis. *See* Musica mundana, humana, instrumentalis

Musica mundana, humana, instrumentalis

Musica mundana, humana, instrumentalis–Mundana

Musical couple (a man and woman, one or both of whom is making music; more than one musical couple is also included in this category)

Musical instruction. *See* Instruction, musical

Musical notation (the notation is legible, or would be if the reproduction were large enough; pseudonotation is not included)

Musical notation–Tablature

Musical source, illustrated (comprises illustrations in manuscript and printed collections of music). *See also* Text, liturgical

Musical term. (To preserve the original as closely as possible, keep the grammatical case in which the term is mentioned. The notation "[lit]" indicates that the term is mentioned in the text but not specifically illustrated by the picture. Check the entire list for variations of the term; the great number of variations in terminology and spelling do not permit cross-referencing.) *See also* Instrument, reference to; Musician, reference to

Musical term–*Buccinate*

> *Buccinate* [lit]
> *Cantate*
> *Canterey* [lit]
> *Canticis* [lit]
> *Cantico* [lit]
> *Canticum*
> *Canticum* [lit]
> *Cantike* [lit]
> *Cantionum* [lit]
> *Cantorey* [lit]
> *Carmen* [lit]
> *Carmina* [lit]
> *Carminis* [lit]
> *Caroles* [lit]
> *Chançun* [lit]
> *Chant* [lit]
> *Chanz* [lit]
> *Charoles* [lit]
> *Choris* [lit]
> *Choro* [lit]
> *Chorus* [lit]
> *Concordantz* [lit]
> *Corneyt*
> *Cwidum* [lit]
> *Ditié* [lit]
> *Fluster* [lit]
> *Junctur* [lit]
> *Karole* [lit]

Musical term–*Lieder* [lit]
        Psalmum [lit]
        Saeng [lit]
        Saitenspill [lit]
        Sang [lit]
        Sealm [lit]
        Simphoney [lit]
        Singaen [lit]
        Singaeþ [lit]
        Singendrae [lit]
        Song [lit]
        Stefne psealmae [lit]
        Tablature [lit]
        ðreaet [lit]
        þrete [lit]
        Trumpant
        Trumpeer
        Vedelede
        Voce carminis [lit]
        Voiz de ditied [lit]
        Voiz de ditiet [lit]
        Zimphonia
Musician, angel. *See* Angel musician; Angel musician, wingless
Musician, animal. *See* Animal musician
Musician in gallery. *See* Gallery, musicians'
Musician, mounted (on a real animal, not a grotesque creature, bird, fish, etc.)
Musician on pedestal. *See* Pedestal, musician on
Musician, reference to. (To preserve the original as closely as possible, keep the grammatical case in which the musician is mentioned. The notation "[lit]" indicates that the term is mentioned in the text but not specifically illustrated by the picture. Check the entire list for variations of the term; the great number of variations in terminology and spelling do not permit cross-referencing.) *See also* Instrument, reference to; Musical term
Musician, reference to–*Cantatores*
        Capelmaister
        Chanteür
        Circulator (peddler)
        Fiedler
        Ganeo (debauchee)
        Lautenschlager
        Ludio Rhutenus (actor)
        Paugker
        Pfeyffer
        Pfeyffer, Burgundisch
        Psallebant
        Psallentibus
        Pusauner
        Reichstrumeter
        Ribeber
        Rybeber
        Sanghers
        Singendum

Office of St. Louis. *See* Text–Hours–Office of St. Louis
Office of the Virgin. *See* Text–Hours
Ofterdingen, Heinrich von. *See* Heinrich von Ofterdingen
Olina, Giovanni Pietro
Olpe, Bergmann von. *See* Bergmann von Olpe
Opera
Opera –Andromeda y Perseo Fabula
Opera–Eta dell'oro, L' (G. F. Tosi)
Opera–Incoronazione di Poppea (Monteverdi)
Opera–Nozze di Theti e di Peleo, Le (C. Caprioli)
Opera–Pomo d'oro, Il (Cesti)
Oraison dominicale, traité sur (treatise on Lord's Prayer)
Orange, William of. *See* William of Orange
Ordinal. *See* Text, liturgical– Ordinal
Oresme, Nicole
Orgeluse (of Arthurian legend)
Orpheus
Orpheus and animals
Orpheus and Eurydice
Orpheus as shepherd
Orsini, Cardinal Pietro
Osma (Spain)
Oswald von Wolkenstein
Otto von Brandenburg, Markgraf
Oureille, Rigault d'
Ovid–Metamorphoses
Padua
Palamedes, Ser, and son Matthew
Palamites
Pamphilus, de amore
Pan
Pandolfini family of Florence
Paradise. *See* Angel musician; Angel musician, wingless; Blessed; Putto musician; Putto
    musician, winged; Virgin–Assumption; Virgin–Coronation; etc.
Parigi, G.
Paris
Paris, Finding of
Paris, Matthew. *See* Chronicle of Matthew Paris
Paris–Place Dauphine
Paris–Place des Vosges
Paris–Tuileries
Parma
Parnassus. *See also* Apollo and Muses; Muses
Part books. *See* Music book
Parzifal
Passau
Passional. *See* Text, liturgical–Passional; names of individual passionals, e.g.,
    Passional of Kunigunde von Böhmen
Passional of Abbess Kunhuta. *See* Passional of Kunigunde von Böhmen
Passional of Kunigunde von Böhmen
Patents of nobility. *See* Text, legal–Patents of nobility
Paul the Hermit

Planets, music associated with—Venus
Planets, The (series)
Platform, musician on. *See also* Pedestal, musician on
Pliny
Plutarch
Pock (fool)
Poet as Creator (shown with his muse, inspiration, or genius, or being adored for his creativity)
Poetry, swan as
Polisy, Lord of. *See* Dinteville, Jean de
Polymnia. *See* Muses—Polymnia
Polyphemus
Pomo d'oro, Il. *See* Opera—Pomo d'oro, Il (Cesti)
Pompey the Great
Pontifical. *See* Text, liturgical—Pontifical; names of individual pontificals
Pontius Pilate. *See* Christ—Before Pilate; Pilate
Pope. *See* names of individual popes
Poverty personified
Praetorius, Michael
Prague
Prenez sur moi vostre exemple. *See* Canon—Prenez sur moi vostre exemple; Chanson—Prenez sur moi vostre exemple
Presentation in the Temple. *See* Christ—Presentation in the Temple
Presle, Raoul de
Priam
Priapus
Priest or priestess. *See* Ceremony, religious—Judaeo-Christian; Ceremony, religious—Pagan; Cleric playing instrument; Cleric singing
Priscus, King
Procession. *See also* Triumph
Procession—Entrée
Procession—Religious. *See also* David—Return of the Ark
Prodigal Son
Pronomos
Prophet. *See* Blessed
Prophetess Anna. *See* Christ—Presentation in the Temple
Prose Tristan. *See* Tristan, Prose
Prudentius
Psalm, Apocryphal. *See* Text—Bible—Psalm 151
Psalms, Book of. *See* Text—Bible—Psalms
Psalmum. *See* Musical term—*Psalmum* [lit]
Psalter. *See* Text—Psalter; names of individual psalters, e.g., Psalter, Bromholm
Psalter, Alfonso
Psalter, Belvoir
Psalter, Bromholm
Psalter, Cambridge
Psalter, Canterbury
Psalter, Eadwine
Psalter, Evesham
Psalter, Hunterian
Psalter, Lothair
Psalter, Louterell. *See* Psalter, Luttrell

Rhetoric. *See* Liberal arts—Rhetoric
Ricasoli, Lisa
Ricercare
Richard, Earl of Cornwall
Richenthal, Ulrich von. *See* Ulrich von Richenthal
Rinuccini, Ottavio
Ritual. *See* Ceremony, religious—Judaeo-Christian; Ceremony, religious—Pagan
Robert de Lindesey, Psalter of. *See* Psalter of Robert de Lindesey
Roccabianca, Castello di
Rocollet, Pierre (publisher/printer)
Rodrígues, Juan de la Cámera. *See* Juan Rodrígues de la Cámera
Roger, le beau
Roland
Roman de Girart de Nevers
Roman de la Rose
Roman de Troie. *See* Bénoit de Sainte-More—Roman de Troie
Roman des chevaliers de la gloire, Le
Romance. *See* Text, literary—Romance or epic; names of individual texts
Romance of Alexander
Rome
Rome—Farnesina house
Rome personified
Rosen, Conrad von der. *See* Conrad von der Rosen
Rossi, Pier Maria
Rot, Conrad von. *See* Conrad von Rot
Rovere, della, family
Rudolph von Ems
Rügenwalder Silberaltar. *See* Altar, Rügenwalder Silber-
Rumslant, Meister
Rustic music (music performed by peasants or in a rural setting). *See also*
    Shepherd musician
Rutland Psalter. *See* Psalter, Rutland
Sabellius
Sacrifice, pagan. *See* Ceremony, religious—Pagan
Saeng. *See* Musical term—*Saeng* [lit]
Sages, The Seven (name for a group of Greek historical characters of the 6th c. B.C.
    famous as propagators of practical worldly wisdom; several lists of them have
    been handed down; a few names occur on all the lists, e.g., Solon, Thales, and
    Pittacus)
Sailor. *See* Ship, music in
Saint. *See also* Blessed; names of individual saints
St. Agnes
St. Albans Psalter. *See* Psalter, St. Albans
St. Andrew
St. Anne
St. Anthony
St. Anthony Abbot
St. Anthony—Temptation
St. Apollonia
St. Architriclin
St. Augustine
St. Augustine Psalter. *See* Psalter, St. Augustine

St. Barbara

St. Bartholomew

St. Benedict

St. Catherine (Not identified further. There are several SS. Catherine. Distinguish among them only when you are sure. Since both St. Catherine of Alexandria and St. Catherine of Siena were mystically married to Christ, do not distinguish between them in the subject entry "St. Catherine–Mystic Marriage" even though it is a subject more commonly associated with Catherine of Alexandria.)

St. Catherine dei Vigri

St. Catherine–Mystic Marriage

St. Catherine of Alexandria

St. Catherine of Siena

St. Cecilia

St. Dominic

St. Dorothy

St. Elizabeth. *See* Virgin–Visitation

St. Erasmus

St. Eulalia

St. Eustace

St. George

St. Giles

St. Hilarion

St. Honoré

St. James the Greater

St. Jerome–Vision

St. John the Baptist. *See also* Christ–Baptism; Herod, feast of

St. John the Evangelist

St. Joseph. *See also* Christ–Flight into Egypt; Christ–Nativity

St. Louis. *See* Louis IX of France; Text–Hours–Office of St. Louis

St. Lucy

St. Luke

St. Luke, Gospel according to. *See* Text–Bible –Luke

St. Margaret

St. Mark

St. Martha

St. Martial

St. Martin

St. Mary. *See* Virgin

St. Mary Magdalene

St. Matthew

St. Matthew, Gospel according to. *See* Text–Bible–Matthew

St. Michael

St. Paul

St. Peter

St. Peter Martyr

St. Ranieri

St. Sebastian

St. Sever, Apocalypse of. *See* Apocalypse of Saint-Sever

St. Severin

St. Stephen

St. Theodelinda

St. Thomas

St. Thomas Aquinas
St. Thomas Aquinas, triumph of. *See* Triumph of St. Thomas Aquinas
St. Thomas(ius) of Costacciaro
St. Ursula
St. Ursula Reliquary. *See* Reliquary, St. Ursula
St. Verdiana
St. Veronica–Veil (sudarium)
St. Vincent
St. Viridiana
St. Wolfgang
St. Wolfgang Altar. *See* Altar, St. Wolfgang
Sainte-More, Bénoît de. *See* Bénoît de Sainte-More
Saitenspill. *See* Musical term–*Saitenspill* [lit]; Instrument, reference to–*Seitenspiel*
Salisbury Breviary. *See* Breviary, Salisbury
Salome. *See* Herod, feast of
Salomon, Jean. *See* Tabarin
Saluzzo Gualtieri, Marchese di. *See* Gualtieri, Marchese di Saluzzo
Samson and Philistines
Samuel. *See* David and Samuel
Samuel, Books of. *See* Text–Bible–Samuel
Sang. *See* Musical term–*Sang* [lit]
Sappho
Satyr (Includes silenus and faun musicians. Satyrs were goat-men like Pan. Sileni were
    part man and part horse; walked on two legs, not four; often had horses' hooves
    instead of feet, sometimes horses' ears, and always horses' tails. Fauns were Roman
    satyrs.) *See also* Centaur
Satyr musician
Saul. *See also* David and Saul
Saxon Chronicle
Sbarra, Francesco
Schatzbehalter, Der
Schedel, Hartmann
Scheidemann, Heinrich
Schlick, Arnold
Schlifer, Nicolaus
Schöffer, Peter, II (publisher/printer)
Schönsperger, Hans (publisher/printer)
School of music. *See* Instruction, musical
Schütz, Heinrich
Schuyt, Cornelius
Schweiger, Jörg
Sciences, theological, personified
Scrope family
Sealm. *See* Musical term–*Sealm* [lit]
Seasons, music associated with–Summer
Séguier family
Selle, Thomas
Selve, George de, Bishop of Lavour
Senfl, Ludwig
Senses, allegory of
Senses, allegory of–Hearing
S'ensuyvent plusieurs basses dances . . .

Soldier. *See* Military subjects
Solmization syllables
Solo musician
Solomon
Solomon and the Queen of Sheba
Solomon, court of
Solomon, judgment of
Song. *See* Musical term–*Song* [lit]
Sophonias, prophet
Spain. *See* Barcelona; Baza; Cadiz; Granada; Madrid; Osma
Spain, Margherita Theresa, Infanta of. *See* Margherita Theresa, Infanta of Spain
Spain, Maria Theresa, Infanta of. *See* Maria Theresa, Infanta of Spain
Spain, Mariana of Austria, Queen of. *See* Mariana of Austria, Queen of Spain
Spanish Chapel. *See* Chapel, Spanish
Sparta
Spechtshart von Reutlingen, Hugo
Spenser, Edmund–The Shepherd's Calendar
Sphinx
Spiegel des menschlichen lebens, Der
Spirit, Holy, Dove of. *See* Holy Spirit, Dove of; Trinity
Splendor personified
Squarcialupi Codex
Squillace, Prince of
Stade
Stadtpfeifer. *See* Civic Music
Stag. *See* Music personified with stag
Stage setting. *See* Theater–Stage setting
Steen, Jan (portrait)
Stefne psealmae. *See* Musical term–*Stefne psealmae* [lit]
Steinach, Bligge von. *See* Bligge von Steinach, Her
Steinen (Germany)
Stephan, P.
Stewdl (trombonist)
Still life, musical
Stoa, Quintinian
Streda, John of. *See* Johann of Neumarkt
Street cry
Street musician (beggars and poor itinerant musicians). *See also* Acrobat or juggler musician; Minstrel; Serenade
Stretlingen, Heinrich von. *See* Heinrich von Stretlingen, Der
Student musician (a student playing music, not to be confused with a music student)
Sudarium. *See* St. Veronica–Veil
Sun. *See* Planets, music associated with– Sun; Sun personified
Sun personified
Suonegge, von
Susanna. *See* Chanson–Susanna
Suso, Heinrich
Swanegoer, Hiltboldt von. *See* Hiltboldt von Swanegoer, Her
Switzerland. *See* Basel
Symposium, ancient Greek, music at
Tabarin, Jean Salomon called
Tablature. *See* Musical notation–Tablature

Tablature. *See* Musical term—*Tablature* [lit]

Tabourot, Jehan. *See* Arbeau, Thoinot

Tabula Cebetis

Tacuinum Sanitatis

Tapestries, History of Abraham

Tapestries, La dame à la licorne

Tapestries, Nine Heroes

Tapestries, Redemption

Tapestries, Seven Deadly Sins

Tapestries, Unicorn

Tapestries, Valois

Tapestry, Credo

Tarocchi cards. *See* Cards, playing—Tarocchi; Tarocchi Cards

Tarocchi Cards (series)

Tavern music (music, solo or ensemble, performed by lower-, middle-, or upper-class musicians in a tavern, a public-room where food and/or drink appears on the table)

Tavernier, Melchior (publisher/printer)

Temperaments—Phlegmatic

Tenison Psalter. *See* Psalter, Tenison

Terence

Terpsichore. *See* Muses—Terpsichore

Text—Bible (complete Bibles, separate Old Testaments, separate New Testaments, Bible commentaries and parts thereof)

Text—Bible—Acts

        Apocrypha. *See* name of chapter, e.g., Text—Bible—Judith

        1 Chronicles

        Esther. *See also* Ahasuerus, feast of

        Exodus

        Genesis. *See also* Jubal; Tubalcain; Adam and Eve; Creation

        Isaiah. *See also* Canticle of Hezekiah (Isaiah 38:10-20)

        Joshua

        Judges

        Judith

        Luke

        Matthew. *See also* Herod, feast of; Oraison dominicale

        Psalms. Illustrations known to be from the Book of Psalms, but whose specific psalm number is not known. The number of the specific psalm illustrated is entered when known. *See also* Text—Psalter, which includes all psalter illustrations, not just those illustrating the psalms.

        Psalm 1

            19 (King James 20)

            21 (King James 22)

            151 (Apocryphal)

            etc.

        Psalms, penitential (Psalms 6, 32, 38, 51, 102, 130, 143, so-called because of the character of their texts)

        Revelation

        1 Samuel [in Vulgate, I Regum]. *See also* David and Saul

        2 Samuel [in Vulgate, II Regum]

Text—Biblical adaptation (includes the Bible historiale, Biblia pauperum, Bible moralisée, versifications of the Bible or versification of parts of the Bible, etc.)

Text–Description of festival

Text, didactic

Text, didactic– Astronomy and astrology

           Calendar (illustrations from sources that are only calendars, not calendars that are parts of larger works). *See also* Months, music associated with (which includes illustrations from various sources such as books of hours, psalters, etc.)

           Chess

           Costumes. *See also* Theater–Costume design

           Dance

           Encyclopedia

           Exemplum (short tales or poems offering moral instruction by example)

           Feminist

           Fine Arts

           Grammar

           Hunting

           Medicine

           Military

           Music

           Natural history

           Natural history–Bestiary

           Topography

           Travel and social customs

Text–Haggadah

Text, hagiographic

Text, historical

Text, historical–Archival records

           Biography

           Chronicle

Text–Hours

Text–Hours–Office of St. Louis

Text, legal

Text, legal– Decretals

           Guild statutes

           Patents of nobility

Text, literary

Text, literary–Drama

           Lyric poetry

           Romance or epic

           Short tales. *See also* Text, didactic–Exemplum

Text, liturgical

Text, liturgical–Antiphonary

           Breviary

           Diurnal

           Gradual

           Lectionary

           Missal

           Ordinal

           Passional

           Pontifical

           Troper

Text, liturgical–Viaticum
Text, philosophical or theological
Text–Psalter
Textless composition. *See* Carmen
Thalassa
Thalia (one of the Three Graces). *See* Graces, Three
Thalia (Muse). *See* Muses–Thalia
Theater–Costume design. *See also* Text, didactic–Costumes
Theater–Costume design–Ballet
              Ballet–*Douairière de Billebahaut, La*
              Commedia dell'arte
              Intermedio
              Opera
Theater–Stage setting. *See also* Intermedio; Opera
Theater–Stage setting–Ballet
              Ballet–*Ballet des Polonaise, Le* (Beaujoyeulx)
              Ballet–*Douairière de Billebahaut*
              Commedia dell'arte
              Intermedio. *See* Intermedio
              Liturgical drama/Mystery play
              Opera. *See* Opera
Theatrical spectacle with music (a dramatic or quasi-dramatic event, e.g., entrée, play, tableau vivant, etc.). *See also* Carrousel; Intermedio; Opera
Theatrical spectacle with music–Ballet. *See* Dancing, theatrical; Theater–Costume design–Ballet; Theater–Stage setting–Ballet
Theatrical spectacle with music–Commedia dell'arte
              Guerra d'amore, La
              Liturgical drama/Mystery play
Theatrical spectacle with music indoors
Theatrical spectacle with music outdoors
Thebes
Theobald, Bishop of Arezzo
Theodolinda, Queen of the Lombards
Theological text. *See* Text, philosophical or theological. *See also* Text–Bible; Text–Hours; Text, liturgical; Text–Psalter
Theology personified
Thetis and Peleus
Thrace
ðreaet. *See* Musical term–ð*reaet* [lit]
þrete. *See* Musical term–þ*rete* [lit]
Throne, Boston
Throne, Ludovisi
Thüringen, Hermann von. *See* Hermann von Thüringen
Thyrsis and Damon
Tickhill Psalter. *See* Psalter, Tickhill
Tiergeville, Pierre de
Time personified. *See also* Triumph of Time
Time, triumph of. *See* Triumph of Time
Title page
Tityrus
Torelli, Giacomo
Torquatus

Tosi, Giuseppe Felice
Tournai. *See* Chevrot, Jean, Bishop of Tournai
Tournament or joust, music at
Tower, arch, gate, wall, etc., musician on
Town band. *See* Civic music
Town musician. *See* Civic music
Treatise, musical. *See* Text, didactic–Music
Tree of Jesse. *See* Jesse Tree
Treibenreif, Peter. *See* Tritonius, Petrus
Très-Belles Heures de Jean duc de Berry. *See* Hours–Très Belles Heures de Jean duc
    de Berry
Trial. *See* Law court
Trieberg (Austria)
Trinity
Trio
Triomphe de l'amour, Le (ballet)
Trionfi. *See* Petrarch–*Trionfi*
Tristan. *See also* Isolde
Tristan, Prose
Tristram. *See* Tristan
Triton musician
Tritonius, Petrus
Triumph of Caesar
Triumph of Church
Triumph of David. *See* David, triumph of
Triumph of Divinity
Triumph of Eucharist
Triumph of Fame
Triumph of Glory
Triumph of Love
Triumph of Maximilian I
Triumph of St. Thomas Aquinas
Triumph of Time
Triumph of Venus
Triumphs of Petrarch. *See* Petrarch–*Trionfi*
Triumphs of Petrarch Tapestries. *See* Tapestries, Triumphs of Petrarch
Troper. *See* Text, liturgical–Troper
Troubadour. *See* Court, music at
Trouvère. *See* Court, music at
Troyes, Chrétien de. *See* Chrétien de Troyes
Trumpant. *See* Musical term–*Trumpant*
Trumpeer. *See* Musical term–*Trumpeer*
Truth personified
Tubalcain (Genesis 4:22). *See also* Jubal
Tuning key
Tuppo, Francesco del (publisher/printer)
Türheim, Ulrich von. *See* Ulrich von Türheim
Türlin, Ulrich von. *See* Ulrich von Türlin
Turberville, George
Turin, Agilulf, Duke of. *See* Agilulf, Duke of Turin
Twelfth Night. *See* Epiphany celebration, music at; Christ–Adoration of the Magi
Ulrich von Richenthal

Virtue and vice, allegory of. *See* Virtues and vices personified
Virtue(s) personified. *See* Virtues and vices personified–Virtues
Virtues and vices personified
Virtues and vices personified–Vices
Virtues and vices personified–Vices–Gula
Virtues and vices personified–Vices–Luxuria
Virtues and vices personified–Virtues
Virtues and vices personified–Virtues–Diuturnitas
Virtues and vices personified–Virtues–Fortitude
Virtues and vices personified–Virtues–Justice
Virtues and vices personified–Virtues–Mercy
Virtues and vices personified–Virtues–Peace
Virtues and vices personified–Virtues–Sanitas
Virtues and vices personified–Virtues–Spes
Virtues and vices personified–Virtues–Velocitas
Virtues and vices personified–Virtues–Voluptas
Visconti family of Pavia
Visitation. *See* Virgin–Visitation
Vitali, Maestro Bernardino de (publisher/printer)
Vittorio Veneto. *See* Ceneda (Vittorio Veneto)
Vivian Bible. *See* Bible, Vivian
Voce carminis. *See* Musical term–*Voce carminis* [lit]
Vogelweide, Walther von der. *See* Walther von der Vogelweide
Voiz de ditied. *See* Musical term–*Voiz de ditied* [lit]
Voiz de ditiet. *See* Musical term–*Voiz de ditiet* [lit]
Vostre, Simon (publisher/printer)
Vulgate Lancelot. *See* Lancelot, Vulgate
Wadley, Berkshire, England
Walther von der Vogelweide
War personified
Warrior. *See* Military subjects
Wedding celebration, music at
Weissenhorn (Austria)
"Weisskunig, Der"
Weltgerichtsaltar. *See* Altar, Weltgerichts-
Wenzel II, King of Bohemia
Westminster Psalter. *See* Psalter, Westminster
Whitehorne, Peter
Whore. *See* Harlot musician
Wild men. *See* Dancing, theatrical–Wild men
Wilhelm V, Duke of Bavaria
Wilhelm von Greyssen
Willehalm. *See* Ulrich von Türheim–Willehalm; Ulrich von Türlin–Willehalm; Wolfram
    von Eschenbach–Willehalm
William of Orange
Winds, four, personified
Wine-making
Winter, Hans (fool)
Winterburger, Joh.
Wisdom personified
Wittemberg
Wolfram von Eschenbach–Willehalm

Wolkenstein, Oswald von. *See* Oswald von Wolkenstein
Women Musicians (Stimmer)
World image
Worthies, Nine. *See* Heroes, Nine
Xantener Altar. *See* Altar, Xantener
Year personified
York Psalter. *See* Psalter, York
Ysolt. *See* Isolde
Zeus
Zeus Hypsistos
Zimphonia. *See* Musical term–*Zimphonia*
Zion
Zodiacal signs
Zodiacal signs–Aquarius
Zweter, Reinmar von. *See* Reinmar von Zweter